# Islam 101:
# Principles and Practice

# Islam 101:
# Principles and Practice

*Arshad Khan*

Khan Consulting and Publishing, LLC
San Jose

**Islam 101:**
**Principles and Practice**

Khan Consulting and Publishing, LLC
PO Box 700012
San Jose, CA 95170
www.khanbooks.com

ISBN: 0-977-2838-36

Printed in the United States of America

# CONTENTS

# TERMINOLOGY

- ❑ ayatollah: Shia religious le.meaning is "sign of God."
- ❑ caliph: Leader of an Islamic polity, regarded as Muhammad$^P$'s successor; the superscript "p" is a short form for "Peace and blessings be upon him" that Muslims recite every time the name of Muhammad$^P$ is invoked.
- ❑ Islam: Religion started by Adam, the first man, and formalized by Muhammad$^P$, the last prophet.
- ❑ jehad: An inner personal struggle to be righteous. In extreme cases, it can involve the laying down of one's life for the right cause, such as the defense of Islam.
- ❑ Kaaba: Cube-shaped structure in Mecca towards which Muslims face when performing their ritual prayers. Built as a place of worship by Prophet Adam and rebuilt by Prophet Abraham.
- ❑ Muhammad$^P$: The prophet who formalized the religion of Islam.
- ❑ Muslim: Person who follows the religion of Islam (one who submits to the will of God).
- ❑ Shia: Minority sect of Islam primarily concentrated in Iran, Iraq and the Indian subcontinent.
- ❑ Sunnah: Actions, sayings, and approvals of Prophet Muhammad$^P$; also referred to as the Hadith.


Note 1:   The Koranic references are denoted in the format (25:32). The first number (25) refers to the chapter while the second number (32) refers to the verse.

Note 2:    The primary readers of this book will be American non-Muslims. Therefore, in consideration of how it is commonly spelled in America, the scripture revealed to Prophet Muhammad has been spelled as Koran, even though Quran is a closer reflection of the way in which it is pronounced in Arabic—the language in which it was revealed.

# INTRODUCTION

The primary objective of *Islam 101: Principles and Practice* is to address the information needs of non-Muslims who are interested in learning about the fastest growing religion in the world—quickly and without being initially encumbered by details. *Islam 101* will also be useful to young Muslims, especially those living in Western societies, who want to learn the basics of Islam.

*Islam 101* covers the fundamental principles, beliefs, and practical aspects of Islam. It covers diverse topics such as morals, good and bad deeds, personal characteristics, rights and obligations, women's rights, Islamic law, sectarian differences, relations with other religions, as well as day-to-day issues. It also indicates how some Muslims, through their practice, have deviated from Islam's true purpose and meaning.

Islam is a way of life that encompasses every aspect of a Muslim's life—personal, social, economic, political, legal, religious, etc. To understand Islam and gain in-depth knowledge about it, one must study its various aspects in greater depth. Therefore, I encourage you to build upon the knowledge gained in this book, and enhance your knowledge of topics that are of interest to you, by mining the Internet and reading some of the many excellent books that are available on the various aspects of Islam.

If you are interested in studying Islamic history and the rise and fall of Islamic power, I suggest that you read my book, *Understanding Muslim-West Alienation: Building a Better Future*, which highlights the reasons for the plight of Muslims in the modern world and also analyzes the factors that cause them to view America and the West so negatively.

# CHAPTER 1
# MUHAMMAD<sup>P</sup>

The religion of Islam, which was started by Prophet Adam, was formalized under the prophethood and leadership of Prophet Muhammad<sup>P</sup>. Muslims are mandated in the Koran, whose teachings they cannot question, to obey him. They are also required to accept all of his rulings with full conviction. Islam instructs Muslims to use his life as a model for living their own day-to-day lives. They are enjoined to emulate everything that he did, minor or significant, in all aspects of his life including personal, social, political, etc. Therefore, in order to understand Islam and Muslims, it is imperative that the life and character of Prophet Muhammad<sup>P</sup> be studied.


# PRE-PROPHETOOD PERIOD

## Birth and childhood

Muhammad<sup>P</sup>, whose ancestry is traced to Prophets Abraham and Ismail, was born in Mecca, Saudi Arabia, in 570. His father, Abdullah ibn Abd al-Muttalib, died before he was born and his mother, Amina, died when he was six years old. Muhammad<sup>P</sup> was raised by his grandfather, Abd al-Muttalib, who belonged to the respected Qureysh tribe. After Abd al-Muttalib's death, Muhammad<sup>P</sup> was raised by his uncle Abu Talib. He never learned to read and write, even though he was born in a leading Meccan family, and remained illiterate till his death.

As a child Muhammad[P] was sent into the desert, as was customary, to live with a Bedouin family for a few years. The tough life of the Bedouins prepared him for the difficult times that he was to face later on in life.

## Life as a youth

Muhammad[P] underwent many experiences during his youth including working in the desert as a shepherd and traveling with a trading caravan to Syria. When he was in his twenties, he was hired by a wealthy widow, Khadijah, to manage her business. His job involved traveling with and managing her trading caravans, which brought him in touch with, and observe, people of different cultures and religions.

Even when he was young, Muhammad[P] did not like, or participate in, the paganism and idol-worship that was prevalent in Arabia at that time. He did not act like most youth and, even at a young age, was highly respected by the people of Mecca due to his personal qualities, especially honesty and trustworthiness. The respect was so high that Muhammad[P] came to be better known as al-Amin (the Honest) and al-Sadiq (The Trustworthy). Due to his exemplary character, he would often be called upon to become the arbiter during disputes.

At the age of 25, Muhammad[P] was approached with a marriage proposal by his 40 year old employer, Khadijah, through an intermediary. He accepted the proposal and they were married in 595. Their marriage lasted till her death in 619, almost 25 years later. The marriage resulted in six children—four daughters and two sons. None of the sons survived past childhood.

## State of Arabia at Muhammad<sup>P</sup>'s birth

When Muhammad<sup>P</sup> was born, Arabia as well as many parts of the world were in a state of moral decay. Arabia, in particular, was in a moral and social abyss characterized by polytheism, idol-worship, ignorance, superstitions, burying alive of new-born girls, tribal conflicts, drinking, injustice, tyranny, lack of women's rights, etc. Their good qualities, like bravery, generosity, confidence and firmness of belief (though wrong), were negated by their vices.

The polytheism and moral decadence of the society around him did not go unnoticed by Muhammad<sup>P</sup>. He contemplated a lot but could not come up with any solution for the negative practices that he observed. Therefore, he remained silent and developed a habit of retreating to Hira, a cave on a hill near Mecca, in order to meditate.

# PROPHETHOOD

## Koran is revealed

At the age of 40, when he was at Hira, Muhammad<sup>P</sup> was approached by the Angel Gabriel, who conveyed to him his first revelation from God. That was followed by many more revelations, which continued till his death in 632. The Koran is the compiled version of those revelations.

The prophethood of Muhammad<sup>P</sup> begins with the first revelation of the Koran in 610. It marks the beginning of his campaign to eradicate all the evils that he had observed among his fellow Arabs. Muhammad<sup>P</sup> managed to get his first convert, his wife Khadijah, right away. However, it took more than two decades for his message to be accepted in practically all of Arabia.

## Preaching in Mecca

Muhammad[P] started to preach Islam to the people of his city, Mecca, after he became a prophet. His attempts were initially met with some amusement and, occasionally, anger. The preaching against their idols upset many Meccans because it repudiated their ancestors' beliefs and also had the potential to severely reduce the large business generated by idol-worshipping pilgrims visiting Mecca.

The character and reputation that Muhammad[P] had developed made many people, especially those who were honest and upright, listen seriously to what he was preaching. Consequently, many people started to convert to Islam. However, there were many, including powerful personalities, who opposed Muhammad[P]. They tried their best to dissuade him from preaching an alien concept—the worship of one God. However, despite opposition that kept increasing, Muhammad[P] continued to preach and conversions continued at a steady pace.

## Basic message and theme

Muhammad[P] basically reiterated the message that the earlier prophets had communicated—that there is only one God and that He alone must be worshipped. He preached that this world is transitionary and that one should prepare for the hereafter and the Day of Judgment. Another fundamental message, though that was not preached during the early days, was that Islam encompassed all spheres of life—not just religious or personal.

Muhammad[P] also preached against prevalent evils and told the Arabs to turn away from:
- Worshipping many gods and idols
- Immorality
- Materialism

❑ Killing of new-born girls
❑ Treating women as chattel (an article of movable personal property)
❑ Tribal in-fighting and revenge
❑ Exploitation and injustice
❑ Superstitions

# PERSECUTION

## Ridicule and threats

The Meccans tried many methods to stop Muhammad[P] from preaching. At first, they tried to dissuade him directly and through his family elders. Next, they tried to ridicule him. When even that failed, they started to use threats. However, even they had no effect on Muhammad[P]. The next step was to boycott him and his followers. The social and economic boycott, by powerful opponents, created a very difficult situation for the prophet and his followers. However, he continued to stand firm despite some very trying times.

## Bribery

Pilgrims from all across Arabia came to Mecca every year to worship at the Kaaba. Therefore, the Meccan pagan leaders became very worried when Muhammad[P] started to speak out against idol-worship and the numerous idols in the Kaaba. They were alarmed at the prospect of losing their idol-worshipping pilgrims if Muhammad[P] were allowed to succeed. Hence, after ridicule and threats failed, they tried another method—bribery. They offered everything that they thought Muhammad[P] might want including leadership, wealth, and kingdom. He responded by saying that he would not forsake his mission, which was commanded by God, even if they put the sun in his right hand and the moon in his left hand. Despite many offers, Muhammad[P] remained steady, turned down all offers that were made, and continued with his preaching.

## Intensified persecution

When all other attempts failed, the Meccans intensified their persecution. Those who joined Islam were humiliated, abused, beaten, tortured, and even killed. The persecution forced some Muslims to seek asylum in Abyssinia, which was ruled by a Christian king. For those who were left behind, the situation in Mecca continued to deteriorate. Even Muhammad[P] himself was not spared physically and, in Taif, he was attacked and physically injured.

## Flight to Medina

Muhammad[P] had been preaching Islam in Mecca with great patience since 610. In 622, he received God's command to emigrate to Medina, a city 260 miles to the north. When the Meccans got wind of his emigration plan, they hatched a plot to assassinate Muhammad[P] in his home. However, he managed to escape the killers and arrived safely in Medina. The migration event is called Hijra and marks the first year of the Islamic calendar.

# DEVELOPMENT OF ISLAMIC SOCIETY

## Islamic state and society are established

Muhammad[P] was welcomed by the people of Medina, many of whom had already accepted Islam during their trips to Mecca. The non-Muslims of Medina were tolerant and more receptive to his message. They provided him with the atmosphere in which he could spread the message of Islam and start to develop an Islamic society. It was in Medina that Muhammad[P] received most of the Koranic revelations that address the political and administrative aspects of Islam.

The move to Medina led to the establishment of the first Islamic society and state over the next ten years. However, the path to their establishment was not easy, even after the migration to Medina, because the Meccans still considered Muhammad[P] to be a threat. Consequently, they did not give up their active opposition to him.

## Continued opposition from Meccans

In Medina, many people converted to Islam, which also started to spread to the surrounding areas. The Meccans soon realized that the new society being setup in Medina would become, with the passage of time, more and more dangerous for them. Therefore, they decided to move militarily against the Muslims.

In 624, the Meccans assembled a large military force and marched towards Medina. The Muslims, who were poorly armed and outnumbered three to one, faced them in a pitched battle at Badr. However, the Meccans were no match for 313 dedicated warriors and suffered a crushing defeat.

The Battle of Badr, a milestone for Muslims, increased their confidence. For the first time, they became conscious of their own power and ability to withstand more powerful forces. That confidence was instrumental in their ability to defeat stronger armies in later years. It was also taken as a sign of divine intervention, which helped to convert many more people to Islam.

The Battle of Badr also made the Muslims' enemies realize that there was a new paradigm in place. They were surprised to observe the Muslims engage in unusual practices. Their abnormal acts included serving better food to war prisoners (than the captors) and releasing a prisoner if he taught an illiterate Muslim how to read and write.

## More battles

The Meccans did not give up after the defeat at Badr. A year later, in 625, they assembled an even larger army of 3,000 warriors and again marched to Medina. This time the battle took place at Uhad. Initially, the Muslims were successful on the battlefield. However, just as victory was in sight, they suffered reverses when some archers prematurely left their positions—thinking that the battle was over. Consequently, many Muslims were killed and the casualties included Muhammad[P]. However, the Meccans again failed to achieve their objective of defeating the Muslims.

Two years later, in 627, the Meccans came back with an army of ten thousand. The Muslims dug a trench around Medina as a protective barrier, which the Meccans were unable to breach. After a failed siege, the Meccans retreated, leaving the Muslims victors in what is known as the Battle of the Trench.

## Return to Mecca

In 628, the Muslims and Meccans signed the treaty of Hudaybiyah, which made the Meccans acknowledge Muhammad[P]'s political authority and also provided some concessions to the Muslims. However, the allies of the Meccans violated the treaty in 630, which caused Muhammad[P] to lead an army of ten thousand to Mecca. The Meccans did not put up a fight and the Muslims captured the city without any loss of life. Muhammad[P] forgave his Meccan enemies, declared an amnesty, and returned to Medina. The remaining Arabian tribes who had not converted to Islam, quickly came into its fold after the fall of Mecca.

In the tenth year of the Hijra, Muhammad[P] made his last pilgrimage to Mecca. There he delivered his farewell sermon in which he stressed the rights of women and the equality of all human beings irrespective of their being black or white, Arab or non-Arab. With the establishment of an Islamic state and society, Muhammad[P]'s mission was accomplished and he died shortly after that in 632—ten years after he had migrated to Medina and less than 23 years since he became a prophet.

# MUHAMMAD[P]'S QUALITIES AND STATURE

## Personality and characteristics

Muhammad[P] was an extraordinary person with many defining qualities and characteristics. He filled many roles including prophet, statesman, legislator, commander, philosopher, teacher, judge, husband, father, and grandfather. He was honest, humble, just, compassionate, kind, considerate, and brave. Muhammad[P] lived an extremely simple life and treated everyone with respect and equality. He practiced what he preached and has been a role model that all true followers of Islam have tried to emulate.

## How Muhammad[P] is viewed by followers of Islam

Muhammad[P], while he is viewed as a prophet and messenger of God, is considered to be just a human being—with none of God's divine attributes. In accordance with the Koranic verse (33:40), which describes Muhammad[P] as the *Seal of the Prophets*, Muslims believe that he is the last prophet in a long line of prophets. For them, Muhammad[P] is not an object of worship. However, they respect him so much that whenever his name is uttered, they add the words "Peace and blessings be upon him."

His life is viewed as the model that all Muslims are expected to emulate, as much as they can, in their day-to-day lives.

## Place in history

Muhammad[P] has been one of the most influential personalities since God created man. He has been the most successful of all religious personalities in this world. He transformed and uplifted a backward and illiterate nation into a united country with high moral standards. He formalized a religion whose 1.2 billion adherents, scattered throughout the world, use his life as the model for living their daily lives. He achieved results that influenced the world in the past and continue to do so now.

In Michael H. Hart's book, *The 100: A Ranking Of The Most Influential Persons In History*, Muhammad[P] has been ranked at the top of the list. According to Hart, "My choice of Muhammad to lead the list of the world's most influential persons may surprise some readers and may be questioned by others, but he was the only man in history who was supremely successful on both the religious and secular levels."

# CHAPTER 2
# BASIC ELEMENTS OF ISLAM

## ISLAM, ALLAH, AND MUSLIMS

### Meaning of Islam

#### *How the word Islam is derived*

The Arabic word "Islam" means "Submission to the will of God." It is derived from the root word "s-l-m", which means "peace." The word Islam, though not the concept, was introduced in the Koran. The concept of Islam is traceable to the first man, Adam, who submitted himself to the will of God. In a broader sense, Islam implies the achievement of peace by submitting totally to the will of God. In the ordinary use of the term these days, Islam refers to the religion that was formalized by Muhammad[P] in Arabia.

Islam's central concept is the oneness of God—belief in a single, supreme, and divine creator—along with the prophethood of Muhammad[P]. Islam is a religion that is not identified with Muhammad[P]'s name—the person who formalized it. In contrast, Christianity is derived from Christ, while Buddhism is named after its founder—Buddha In the case of Islam, its name is associated with God. Hence, misnomers like Muhammadanism are considered offensive by Muslims. According to Islam, despite his status as a prophet, Muhammad[P] is not divine and must not be worshipped. Muslims do not pray to him or through him.

11

### What submission implies

The concept of submission requires that a person must submit to God completely, sincerely and willingly. In practice, it means that one should obey all of God's commandments and live according to His law. His basic commands and guidance, which were revealed through His various prophets, are:

☐ There is no deity but God
☐ He is one, unique, and sovereign
☐ He is the only one worthy of worship and obedience
☐ Only through submission and surrender to God, and actively obeying His commands and laws, can one live in peace and attain salvation
☐ Submission makes a man aware of his place in the universe, God's sovereignty, and his obligation to Him
☐ Submission entails recognizing and submitting to God's plan

## Allah

Allah is the Arabic word for God. It is derived from two words: *al* (the) and *ilah* (God). Therefore, it literally means *The God*, which implies "The one and only God." Arabic speaking Christians and Jews also use the word Allah when referring to God. In Aramaic, a language that Jesus also spoke, the word Allah is used for God. In principle and concept, there is no difference between Allah and God. Contrary to some misconceptions among non-Muslims, Allah is:

☐ Everyone's God
☐ The One and Only God
☐ Not some idol or creature that the followers of Islam pray to
☐ The same God that Christians and Jews believe in and worship

The word Allah, which is the personal name of God, has some unique characteristics. It has no plural or gender in the Arabic language. Its other defining characteristics are:

- ❏   He is the only God
- ❏   He begets not nor is He begotten
- ❏   There is none like Him

There are ninety nine attributes of God that are mentioned in the Koran and Hadith. It is through these names that Muslims try to get to know and understand God. The names include The All-Merciful, The All-Knower, The Protector, The Provider, and The Helper.

## Who is a Muslim

Muslim is an Arabic word that means "a person who submits." It refers to a person who follows Islam and submits to the will of God. In Western countries, Muslims are referred to as Moslems. Muslims consider Adam, the first prophet, to be the first Muslim because he was the first follower of Islam. They also view all other prophets as Muslims because they also submitted to God and followed His commandments.

The basic criteria for joining Islam is simple. In principle, the moment someone rejects the worship of everyone except God, he becomes a Muslim. The formal procedure for becoming a Muslim involves making the formal declaration of faith, "There is no god except God and Muhammad[P] is the messenger of God." This declaration implies belief in God with all His attributes, His messengers, their messages, and all the scriptures that they brought. Once formal entry has been made through the declaration of faith, Islam requires that one become God-conscious and, till death, continuously choose between right and wrong.

Muslims do not believe in the concept of original sin. They believe that Adam was forgiven by God when he prayed for pardon and that every child is born free from sin. Also, when someone becomes a Muslim, sincerely, all his previous sins are forgiven and he starts a new life with a clean record. However, while such a person becomes eligible for paradise after becoming a Muslim, he remains accountable for all his future actions.

While the declaration of faith is simple, it requires sincerity. Its recitation leads to an obligation to meet the following requirements:
- Worshipping no one except God
- Always distinguishing between the Creator and His creations
- Fulfilling the rights of God
- Following a life based on the five pillars of Islam:
    o Declaration of faith
    o Praying five times a day
    o Fasting during the month of Ramadan
    o Giving charity
    o Performing the Hajj pilgrimage
- Choosing between right and wrong
- Fulfilling the rights of human beings
- Accepting the fundamental beliefs of Islam
- Implementing Islam's moral and ethical standards of living

# BACKGROUND AND TEACHINGS

## Islam builds upon the older religions' teachings

These days, reference to Islam means the final form of Islam preached by Muhammad[P]. However, Muslims do not consider it to be a new religion started by him. They view it as the final version of a religion whose basic principles and roots go back to Adam—the first man and the first prophet. Ever since Adam, various prophets and messengers have reiterated the same basic message of God's oneness to their people.

According to Hadith, there were about 124,000 prophets, of which 25 are mentioned in the Koran including Abraham, Noah, Moses, and Jesus. According to the Koran, "And every nation had a messenger (10:47)." The message delivered by the prophets, while tailored in some regions as per the requirements of the time that it was delivered, retained the basic and fundamental concept—submission to God.

Muslims believe that the last, and what is considered to be the perfect, message was delivered by Muhammad[P] in the seventh century. Muhammad[P] is viewed as the final prophet of Islam during whose time the religion was perfected. Therefore, he will not be followed by any more prophets. The basis for such a belief is the Koranic verse, "This day have I perfected your religion for you, completed My favor upon you, and have chosen for you Islam as your religion (5:3)."

## Basic message and teachings

The basic message of Islam is that God is one, unique and sovereign. He is distinctly separate from His creations and that only He, and not His creations, should be worshipped. Worshipping any of God's creations, either directly or indirectly, or attributing His qualities to them is a cardinal sin in Islam.

A Muslim is expected to seek, in every aspect of his life, God's pleasure by obeying His commandments and following His guidance. Some of the basic teachings that Muslims are expected to be aware of, or practicing, include:
- ❏ Live in accordance with God's laws
- ❏ Live a God-conscious life

❑ Strive to come close to God as all beliefs and practices are geared to meet this objective
❑ This world is just a preparation for the hereafter
❑ God rewards and punishes in this world and in the hereafter
❑ Be satisfied with what God has given us
❑ Each person is responsible for his or her own actions
❑ Make a conscious effort to overcome temptations; control passions and desires
❑ God accepts sincere repentance
❑ Satan drives people to sin
❑ There is no intermediary between God and man
❑ Exhibit high moral qualities and characteristics such as honesty, integrity, patience, humility, etc.
❑ Be socially responsible
❑ All humans are equal without regard to race, class or gender
❑ There is no demarcation between religion and state (or politics)
❑ Participate in worldly affairs in addition to religious obligations
❑ Everything good for spiritual and physical health is permitted while anything harmful is prohibited

## Fundamental beliefs

The fundamental beliefs that Muslims must accept unconditionally are the following:
❑ Belief in God with all His attributes and qualities
❑ Belief in angels
❑ Belief in divine scriptures—the books of God
❑ Belief in prophets and messengers
❑ Belief in the Day of Judgment—when everyone will have to account for their actions in this world
❑ Belief in divine decree or pre-ordainment—everything that takes place in this world only happens with God's knowledge; He controls human destiny

## Purpose of human life and man's responsibilities

According to the Koran, God created man as His vicegerent or ambassador on earth—the highest level among creations (2:30). The earth and everything in it was created for man's benefit. A Muslim believes that man's life has a purpose beyond physical needs and material activities. The objective is to worship and obey God because man was created for that very purpose. The goal is to attain the best of both worlds: on earth and in the hereafter. However, that does not imply becoming a hermit in perpetual meditation. It means to worship Him, know Him, and to implement His commands and laws in all aspects of life, while carrying on a normal day-to-day life.

As God's ambassador, man has certain responsibilities that need to be discharged. He has to fulfill the purpose of his existence and implement God's plan on earth. To help him, God has provided intelligence and the freedom to choose, which entails responsibility as well as reasoning power. Therefore, if he fails to follow God's commandments and His message, and commit wrong deeds, he will be unable to discharge his responsibilities and, consequently, be held accountable. Hence, to help and guide man, God sent many prophets since the beginning of time.

## Rewards and punishments

Islam clearly indicates the rewards and punishments that man can expect, by following or straying from the right path, in this world as well as in the hereafter. The obedient ones can expect to be rewarded for their good deeds while those committing bad deeds can expect to be punished. According to the Koran, "On the day when every person will be confronted with all the good he has done and all the evil he has done, he will wish that there were a great distance between him and his evil (3:30)."

For some deeds, the punishment to be meted out in this world are clearly spelled out. They include crimes such as murder, stealing and adultery. However, even if a person escapes the punishment for such crimes and other transgressions in this world, there will be no escape on the Day of Judgment. For Muslims, such a belief becomes a great incentive to fear God's punishment and, therefore, try to be good in this world and follow His commandments.

## Salvation

According to Islam, for God to accept deeds that will lead to salvation, the following conditions must be met:
❑   Belief in God and His oneness
❑   Faith and deeds must be based on sincerity and true convictions—not compulsion or blind following
❑   They must be in accordance with Islamic teachings, as mentioned in the Koran and taught by Muhammad[P]

On the Day of Judgment, God will judge every man and woman based on their beliefs, thoughts, deeds, and adherence to, or rejection of, His commandments and laws. Those who reject His message and commands, will not attain salvation. They will be sent to hell where unbelievers and sinners will be placed till eternity. To attain salvation, one has to believe in God, follow His injunctions, and combine beliefs and practice. The determination of whether a person goes to heaven or hell will be made by God, who alone knows about every act and deed committed by that person. He will be the ultimate judge who will decide the fate of every person.

# IMPORTANT ELEMENTS DEFINING ISLAM

## More than a religion: A way of life

Islam is more than a religion. While its foundation is the belief in one God and obedience of His commands, which are central to everything else, Islam is actually a complete way of life for its followers—from cradle to grave. It extends beyond the performance of some rituals to encompass all spheres of life including:

- Spiritual and religious
- Personal
- Family
- Moral
- Ethical

- Political
- Social
- Economic
- Business
- Legal

Islam's tenets and rules cover individuals, societies, as well as governments. They provide guidance in dealing with and treating others including family members, relatives, society, and other nations. They also teach how to live one's daily life and prepare for the hereafter.

## Universal appeal

Entry into Islam, which tries to reach out to all human beings, is not restricted as in Judaism. Acceptance into the Islamic fold is not restricted to Arabs, some chosen people, or a particular nation or tribe. Islam rises above race, ethnicity, gender, color, nationality, social standing, and other narrow considerations. It is also not restricted to any period in time. The message, delivered by Muhammad[P], is supposed to be final and, hence, eternal. Its principles and laws are not subject to change now or in the future.

Islam exhorts Muslims to consider other Muslims as brothers and sisters. That teaching effectively breaks down boundaries across countries. Islam makes Muslims in all parts of the world think of Muslims in foreign countries, who share the same beliefs, as being in the same brotherhood or Ummah.

Islam is a religion that is followed by 1.2 billion Muslims who are scattered all over the world in practically every continent and country. Arabs make up only 22 percent of the total Muslim population though some sources indicate that this number is even lower—about 18 percent. This low figure is contrary to the widely held belief among non-Muslims that Muslims are primarily Arabs. In fact, there are almost as many Muslims in just two Asian countries, Pakistan and India, than in all the Arab countries combined.

## Rigid on fundamental principles

The basic principles of Islam are inviolable and no human being has the authority to change them. According to Islam, anything that is revealed in the Koran, which is the primary source of Islamic laws, cannot be deviated from and must be obeyed without question. They include all the do's and the don'ts. Besides the Koran, Muslims are required to follow the sayings and practice of Muhammad[P]. They are mandated to follow him through God's commandment in the Koranic verse, "We sent not a messenger, but to be obeyed, in accordance with the will of Allah (4:64)."

Islam strongly discourages any innovations, called Bid'ah in Arabic, in its laws, principles or practice—such as the acts of worship. It does not accept the starting of something new, as part of the religion, unless there is a basis for it in the Koran or Sunnah. Innovation restrictions extend to both additions and deletions. A person who makes any changes to God's mandated laws is considered to be committing polytheism, which is considered a grievous sin in Islam. However, innovations in science, technology, medicine, and other fields are encouraged.

## Flexible

While Islam is very rigid regarding basic principles, beliefs, and practices, it does permit a fair amount of flexibility. As a general principle, if something has not been specifically prohibited, either by the Koran or by Muhammad[P], it is permissible. Islam allows new laws to be made, to deal with change and progress, so long as they do not conflict with fundamental Islamic principles and rules, established beliefs and practices (such as fasting and prayers), or established rules and regulations for marriage, inheritance, etc.

## Practical and balanced

Contrary to the general view among non-Muslims, Islam supports a balanced and middle road—not extremes. It attempts to strike a balance between the requirements of this world and the next. The Koran says, "Seek, with the (wealth) which Allah has bestowed on thee, the Home of the Hereafter, nor forget thy portion in this world (28:77)."

Islam, in contrast to the formalism of Judaism and spirituality of Christianity, encourages man to have the best of both worlds. It encourages balance in various aspects of life. It does not encourage one to be either a spendthrift or a miser. Islam encourages marriage rather than celibacy. It allows people to accumulate wealth while mandating charity for those who have the means and assets. Islam mandates justice for both Muslims and non-Muslims, rulers and their subjects, as well as for rich and poor people.

## Common misconceptions about Islam

The following are some common misconceptions about Islam:

❑ Islam supports customs such as forced marriages, denial of education to girls, and genital mutilation: These are tribal and cultural practices that are not supported by Islam.

❑ Islam does not support human rights: This is not true as Islam supports them very strongly.

❑ Islam is against democracy: This is not true; only laws that are implemented against Islamic Law and God's commands are not supported.

❑ Women are inferior to men: This is false. Islam considers all humans equal, with their final destination being determined by their righteousness—not their gender.

❑ Muslims do not believe in God or Jesus: This is false. Muslims believe in God since it means the same as Allah. However, Muslims do not believe that Jesus was the son of God. Muslims are required to believe in Jesus but only as a prophet.

❑ Islam condones terrorism: This is false. According to the Koran, the killing of one innocent human is equivalent to the killing of all mankind.

❑ Islam is intolerant: This is false. Islam enjoins that there is no compulsion in religion. Non-Muslim citizens of an Islamic state are free to practice their religion and the safety of their life and property is guaranteed.

❑ Islam is racist: This is false. According to Islam, all people on earth are equal.

❑ Nation of Islam is a part of Islam: This is false. Nation of Islam has many fundamental principles that Islam rejects completely such as considering a human being, Wallace Fard, as God incarnate. The Nation of Islam espouses principles, such as the superiority of blacks, that are in complete contradiction with the teachings of Islam.

# SYMBOLS AND FESTIVALS

## Spiritual centers

### *Mecca*

Mecca, which is located in western Saudi Arabia, is the religious and spiritual center of Islam. The reasons for its importance are:

❑ Islam started in Mecca, where Muhammad[P] started to receive the Koranic revelations
❑ It is the site of the Kaaba:
  o towards which Muslims, throughout the world, face when offering their ritual prayers
  o which is the symbol of unity and equality for Muslims throughout the world
❑ It is the place where Hajj is performed

The Kaaba was built as a place of worship by Abraham and his son Ishmael. It has been rebuilt many times since then. Pilgrims performing the Hajj are required to circle the Kaaba. In recent years, its surrounding area, which is part of the Grand Mosque of Mecca, has been expanded considerably to accommodate the rising number of pilgrims. At one corner of the Kaaba is the Black Stone, believed to be a meteor, which pilgrims attempt to touch or kiss when they circle the Kaaba. The belief is that Abraham placed it in the Kaaba as a sign of God's affection. According to Islamic belief, the reward of one prayer inside this mosque equals the reward of 100,000 prayers in any other mosque.

## *Medina*

Medina, which is the Muslims' second holiest site, provided refuge to Muhammad[P] when he had to flee Mecca due to persecution. It is located near the historic Badr and Uhad battlegrounds where Muslims won their first victories against the Meccans. The Masjid Nabavi mosque, built by Muhammad[P], is also located in Medina. Its subsequent expansion caused it to encompass Muhammad[P]'s home, where he was buried upon his death. According to Islamic belief, the reward of one prayer in Masjid Nabavi equals the reward of 50,000 prayers in any other mosque.

At Medina the first Islamic society and state came into existence. The city's other significance is that customarily, after the completion of the Hajj pilgrimage requirements, many pilgrims visit Medina for a few days even though it is not a ritual or mandated requirement.

## *Jerusalem*

Jerusalem is the third most important city for Muslims. It is the city where many prophets preached and, consequently, is considered a spiritual symbol by many religions including Islam. It is also the site of the al-Aqsa mosque from where Muhammad[P] ascended to Heaven for a brief visit in 620. In that journey, undertaken in a single night, Muhammad[P] traveled from Mecca to Heaven, via Jerusalem, and then back to Mecca.

# Islamic calendar

The Islamic calendar starts from 622—the year in which Muhammad[P] migrated to Medina. It is called Hijra, which means migration, and is lunar based. Each of the 12 lunar months are either 29 or 30 days long. A new month starts whenever the new moon is sighted. Since a lunar year is about 11 days shorter than the solar year, the Islamic calendar cycles through the various seasons. The Islamic months are Muharram, Safar,

Rabi al-Awwal, Rabi al-Thani, Jumada al-Awwal, Jumada al-Thani, Rajab, Shaaban, Ramadan, Shawwal, Dhu al-Qidah and Dhu al-Hijjah.

The sighting of the moon is an important event for Muslims. It determines the start of Ramadan fasting, the celebration of various festivals such as the two Eid holidays, and the start of the Hajj pilgrimage.

## Festivals and religious days

### Festivals

The two most important religious festivals for Muslims are:
- Eid al-Fitr (celebration of fast breaking)
- Eid al-Adha (celebration of sacrifice)

Eid al-Fitr marks the end of Ramadan—the month during which Muslims fast every day from dawn till sunset. It falls on the first day of Shawwal and is marked by an early morning congregational prayer followed by celebrations and feasting. Relatives and friends are visited on the day of Eid al-Fitr while children are given gifts or cash.

Eid al-Adha commemorates Prophet Abraham's attempted sacrifice of his son when he was commanded by God to do so. It also marks the end of the Hajj pilgrimage, which falls on the tenth day of Dhu al-Hijjah. On that day, an early morning congregational prayer is offered. After the prayer, Muslims visit their relatives and friends. The highlight of the Eid al-Adha festival is the animal sacrifice. Every family that can afford it sacrifices an animal which, typically, is a goat, lamb, cow or camel. The sacrificed animal's meat is distributed to relatives and poor people.

## Lailat al-Qadr

Lailat al-Qadr, or the night of power, falls on one of the last ten nights of Ramadan. It is generally believed to fall on the 27<sup>th</sup> of Ramadan. In 610, on Lailat al-Qadr night, Muhammad[P] received his first revelation of the Koran. Muslims celebrate that historical event by staying up most of the night offering special prayers and reciting the Koran.

## Congregational day: Friday

There is a special, mandatory, congregational prayer offered in mosques every Friday around mid-day. It is marked by a short speech, called a Khutba, by a religious leader or the mosque imam. The Muslim Friday service is somewhat similar to the Sunday service for Christians. Some Muslim countries use Friday as the weekend holiday instead of Sunday .

# CHAPTER 3
# THE SIX BELIEFS

## BELIEF IN ONE GOD

### Core concept: Oneness of God

The core and fundamental concept in Islam is the oneness of God or "Tawheed" in Arabic. According to Islam, God is the creator and sustainer of this universe and, for those who believe it, His supremacy provides a rational explanation for the existence of this complex universe.

The belief in God can be described in different ways:
- ❑ He is divine and unique in every way; He has no partner or son
- ❑ He is the most merciful and the most beneficent
- ❑ He is self-sufficient and supreme
- ❑ He is eternal, infinite and mighty
- ❑ He is merciful and compassionate
- ❑ His knowledge encompasses the whole universe
- ❑ He is all-hearing, all-seeing, and all-knowing; He knows what is apparent and what is hidden as well as the past, present, and future
- ❑ He is the only one who is worthy of being worshipped; no one else has that right
- ❑ He is accessible to all; anyone can approach Him directly without any intermediary
- ❑ He has no physical form or attributes
- ❑ He is the law-giver and judge

- ❏ He loves those who obey Him, forgives those who repent, and does not punish unjustly
- ❏ Nothing can happen in this world without His will
- ❏ He has complete authority over life, death, and destiny—both good and bad
- ❏ He is the one who can restore after death

## Unconditional acceptance

According to Islam, God expects total and unconditional acceptance of His commandments and laws from man of his own free will. Man is the only creation to whom He has given:
- ❏ A mind that can think
- ❏ Freedom of choice

The freedom that has been granted to man puts him in a position where he has to decide whether to be a slave to God's creations and his own desires or to Almighty God.

In Islam, there is no room for legislating laws that, in any way, conflict with or supercede God's laws. He has not given anyone the right to suspend, cancel or change His laws. Anyone who attempts to do that is in conflict with the basic concept of God's supremacy. Consequently, according to Islam, such a person commits the serious sin of equating himself with God.

# BELIEF IN ANGELS

## Who are the angels

Belief in angels is a basic Islamic belief. Angels are God's creations who simply follow God's commands in a very precise way. The most famous angel is Gabriel, who is also known as the angel of revelation. He was responsible for carrying God's commandments and messages to the various prophets and messengers. His last such duty was in revealing the Koran to Muhammad[P]. Gabriel also announced to Mary, the mother of Jesus, that she would be expecting a child—the Messiah being awaited by the Israelis.

Every living person has two angels on duty at his side at all times. One of them records his good deeds and the other one records his bad deeds or sins. According to Islam, all of a person's deeds will be presented and weighed, good versus bad, on the Day of Judgment. Other important angels are the:
- Angel of death, who makes his appearance when a person is about to die
- Angel who will blow the horn on the Day of Judgment
- Angel who is responsible for nature (sun, moon, rain, galaxy, etc.)

## Attributes and tasks

Angels are strictly spiritual entities that do not need any food, drink or rest. They do not have any physical needs and are constantly serving and worshipping God. They only obey God's commands and act as messengers to His prophets, meting out His punishments and other tasks. In contrast to humans, angels are intelligent beings. However, they do not possess the free will to act as they like. While Muslims are expected to respect them, angels are not to be worshipped.

# BELIEF IN GOD'S REVEALED BOOKS

## Belief in divinely revealed scriptures

A divinely revealed scripture is a book, or collection of writings, that has been revealed by God. Many scriptures were revealed over time, to various prophets, with the objective of communicating God's command's and guidance to a particular nation, tribe or group of people. Islam teaches that all the scriptures must be respected and believed in. A Muslim cannot be considered as one unless he believes in all of them.

Angel Gabriel was used by God to communicate with all the prophets and reveal the various scriptures. The only exception was in the case of Moses with whom God communicated directly.

## Scriptures that a Muslim believes in

God revealed many scriptures to his various messengers over thousands of years. As part of their beliefs, Muslims believe in those scriptures as being the actual word of God. The scriptures mentioned in the Koran include the following:

- ❑ Scrolls revealed to Abraham
- ❑ Torah (Taurat) revealed to Moses
- ❑ Psalms (Zaboor) revealed to David
- ❑ Gospel (Injeel) revealed to Jesus
- ❑ Koran (Quran) revealed to Muhammad[P]

The Koran was revealed by Angel Gabriel to Muhammad[P] in parts over a lengthy period stretching from 610 to 632. The verses that were revealed during that period had many objectives including issuing God's commandments and laws, providing historical examples (of rewards and punishments), responding to the current situation or needs of the Muslim community, provide advice, lift morale, act as a guide, etc.

## Belief that pre-Koran scriptures have been corrupted

While Muslims believe in the original scriptures that were revealed to the various messengers before the Koran, they do not believe that their currently available versions are authentic. They believe that, over time, the original scriptures were subject to additions, deletions, changes, and distortions. Many of them were carried out intentionally by those seeking to benefit from the changes. Consequently, Muslims believe that the scriptures currently available consist of the original divine revelations as well as new materials that were authored by men. Hence, due to the unavailability of any copies of the original scriptures, it is impossible to identify the genuine and doctored parts of a particular scripture. Therefore, they cannot be used with any confidence.

The Koran is the last scripture that was revealed, in Arabic, by God. It reaffirms the fundamental principles contained in the previous scriptures. The Koran is still available in the exact version in which it was revealed to Muhammad[P] without even a single punctuation change. Since the older scriptures currently available are not considered authentic, Muslims only follow the Koran.

# BELIEF IN PROPHETS AND MESSENGERS

## Who were the prophets and messengers

The prophets were the chosen people of God who received revelations from Him. They, in turn, had to convey His message to their people. The prophets, who numbered about 124,000, were sent to every nation throughout the world. Their common message was monotheism, how to live righteously in accordance with God's commandments and laws, and how to attain salvation. The prophets were not sent to predict the future.

Muslims are required to believe in every prophet sent by God. The most important ones who have been identified in the Koran are Adam, Noah, Abraham, Jesus, and Muhammad[P]. A messenger is a special type of prophet—one to whom a book of God has been revealed. Some of the messengers, called rasool in Arabic, include Moses, David, Jesus, and Muhammad[P]. A nabi is a prophet to whom a scripture was not revealed.

According to Islam, all the prophets were Muslims. They were humans and none had God's divine qualities or attributes. They cannot be worshipped nor can supplication be made to them because such activities are considered polytheist.

## Purpose and common message

Man was created by God so that he would worship Him and lead a life of virtue. God's expectation from man has been that he would base his life on His guidance, commandments, and laws. In order to make the people who were required to worship Him aware of His commands and laws, God sent His prophets to every nation with clear instructions and guidance.

A very important objective of the prophets was to connect human beings to their creator. Their common message was the call to worship only God, without any partners, and to submit to Him completely. Those who rejected their message became disbelievers. While some laws brought by the various prophets were different, there was no difference in their basic teachings, principles, and message. The prophets also had an important task of issuing warnings of punishments to be meted out, in this world as well as in the next, for those who disobeyed God. In addition, they brought news of rewards for those who obeyed God's commandments and laws.

## How Muslims regard other prophets

All the prophets and messengers, who came periodically to renew the message, were men of high character who preached the same eternal message. Therefore, Muslims respect all of them without any exception. They do not reject any messenger like the Christians who rejected Muhammad[P] or the Jews who rejected Jesus. In fact, Muslims are the only ones who consider belief in all the prophets an article of faith.

## Muhammad[P]'s role as the last prophet

In some cases, a message brought by a prophet changed earlier messages to reflect changes in society due to the passage of time. However, the basic message of all the earlier prophets remained the same—oneness of God and life after death. Muhammad[P] was sent to confirm the earlier messages brought by the various prophets. He also had to remove deviations, that had crept into the message over time, and rectify the lifestyle deterioration that had crept into society.

Muhammad[P], the last messenger of God, is known as the seal of the prophets. According to Islam, he delivered the complete and final message that all future generations are expected to follow. Although Muslims believe in all the prophets and messengers, they are required to follow the specific message delivered by Muhammad[P] who gave mankind one message, a complete code of life, and made Islam a universal religion. According to Islam, no prophet will follow Muhammad[P]. Therefore, anyone claiming to be a prophet after him is considered to be an imposter.

Muslims are expected to follow two sources of guidance in their lives. The first is the Koran—the word of God. They are also required to emulate Muhammad^P's lifestyle in every phase of their life, wherever it can be incorporated.

# BELIEF IN THE DAY OF JUDGEMENT

## Life and death

Islam teaches that life and death are in God's hands. He has appointed a specific time for everyone to transition from life to death. The fact that death is inevitable is constantly referred to in the Koran. When the news of someone's death is heard, Muslims are taught to say, "From God we come and to God we go" and to accept God's decree. Even though the loss and grief of a loved one may last for a very long time, outward mourning is required to end after three days.

Islam teaches that man's present life on earth is only a temporary phase, which has been described as "cultivation of the hereafter." It is a test, where one gets prepared, for life in the hereafter—which will continue forever. Every individual has to go through this very important trial preparation and test. Therefore, Islam teaches that one should prepare for the ultimate destination by living a good life on earth and following God's commandments.

## Day of Judgment

According to Islam, just like Christianity, the universe will be destroyed on the Day of Judgment. On that day, the dead will be resurrected, the soul will be reunited with the body, and all human beings will have to answer for everything that they did during their life on earth. Their fate and future happiness, or unhappiness, will be decided based upon their beliefs and deeds on earth.

The deeds to be judged by God include intentions, thoughts, words spoken, and actions taken throughout the course of one's life. Those whose good deeds outweigh the bad deeds will be rewarded with admittance to heaven, where they will stay forever. However, hell will be the destination of those whose bad deeds predominate. Among those who have been promised hell are the unbelievers, polytheists, and hypocrites.

On the Day of Judgment, when the dead will be raised from their graves and rejoined with their souls, there will be no escape for anyone. No lawyers, wealth or arguments will enable anyone who has done bad deeds to get out of trouble. On the other hand, those who were never rewarded on this earth, despite leading exemplary lives, will be acknowledged and compensated through admittance to heaven.

## Benefit of having accountability

For man, there is a great benefit in knowing that there is ultimate accountability and life after death. It makes life more meaningful. A person knows that trials, tribulations, and present difficulties are only temporary. Therefore, if he continues to perform good deeds and obey God, he will ultimately be a winner and go to heaven. Such a belief makes it easier to lead a virtuous life on earth. It helps protect against a host of evils and sins such as dissatisfaction, crime, corruption, dishonesty, injustice, etc.

## Life after death

When a person dies, his soul is separated from the body and, later, it is reunited with the body when it is laid in the grave. There the angels question him and ask him to identify his Lord—which will mark him as a believer or a non-believer.

After death, a Muslim's body is first washed, wrapped in a clean white shroud, and buried after a funeral prayer. While the buried body decomposes into dust after some time, the soul continues to live on. It will remain passive till the Day of Judgment when resurrection will occur and accountability will take place. Life in the hereafter will be real, spiritual as well as physical, and one will live with both body and soul.

According to Muhammad[P], the following acts continue to help a Muslim even after death:
❑   Charity that the deceased has given
❑   Knowledge that he has left behind (taught, wrote, etc.)
❑   Prayers on his behalf by his children, relatives, friends or others
❑   Actions of a righteous child or student

## Paradise and Hell

Only God knows the real nature and description of heaven and hell. In the Koran, heaven is described as a place of gardens and rivers where all the desires of a person can be satisfied. In heaven, no evil or sickness will exist and every wish will be granted. However, hell is described as a horrible and torturous place engulfed by fire where a person will suffer indefinitely. According to Muhammad[P]'s description of hell, "There are things which no eye has ever seen, no ear has ever heard, and no mind has ever conceived." Hence, based on these descriptions, man can expect his reward or punishment in the hereafter to be extreme.

# BELIEF IN PRE-ORDAINMENT (al-QADAR)

## Fate and divine decree

The sixth Islamic article of faith is belief in God's decree, al-Qadar, or pre-ordainment. It means that nothing can happen anywhere in the universe without the will of God. Anything that does takes place, good or bad, happens as God ordains it. Although man may think, according to his human capabilities, that events occur due to some immediate cause(s), their occurrence is actually due to the wish of God. However, although God has the supreme authority, He has granted human beings flexibility and authority that enables them to make appropriate choices and exercise judgment.

The belief in divine decree is based on the following:
- God knows everything about the past, present, and future due to His infinite knowledge
- God has recorded everything that is going to occur until the Day of Judgment
- Everything that happens takes place according to God's Will
- God created everything

In Islam, a person who believes in God from the depth of his heart is called a *Mumin*—a person who has faith or *Iman*. Every Muslim is expected to strive to become a Mumin, whose attitude is reflected in his actions. For example, a Mumin will not:
- Permit difficulties to weigh him down and cause depression; instead, he will try his best to change the adverse situation and then be patient if he does not succeed despite his best efforts—realizing that it was divine decree

❑ Ask God for something specific; rather, he will ask God for whatever is best for him in both the worlds because God, and not man, knows what really is best for him

## Free will and the ability to choose right or wrong

al-Qadar does not rule out the existence of free will. Islam does not want man to believe that he is being forced to make wrong decisions because everything is ordained and God has knowledge of everything. According to Islam, man has been given free will by God and, hence, he is free to choose between good and evil or right and wrong. No one is forced to make a decision—right or wrong. Therefore, whatever man chooses to do is his own responsibility.

A sinner cannot use al-Qadar as an excuse. The reason is that he commits sins by his own free will. A sinner has no knowledge of what God has decreed for him since no one can know what God has decreed till it actually happens. Therefore, he cannot justify his actions by saying that God decreed it.

According to Islam, God has made His own master plan. However, that must not make one a fatalistic or prevent one from making his own plans. Muslims are encouraged to plan and choose when presented with various options. However, if their plans do not work out despite their best efforts, they are not expected to lose faith. In case of failure, they are encouraged to accept the fact that the results were not reached despite their best efforts due to the will of God and, therefore, they should try to be satisfied with the result even though it was not desired.

## How belief in al-Qadar is beneficial

The belief in al-Qadar brings peace of mind, especially during bad times. For example, if an undesirable result occurred, as a consequence of one's act, the person is assured that it only happened because it was ordained. Such a view prevents grieving about what happened. Instead, the person is more concerned about the act being good because he wants to be rewarded by God at some stage.

The al-Qadar belief also brings humility and modesty. It makes a Muslim realize that success is only achieved because God helped and willed it. If He had wanted to, God could have prevented that success. It also provides confidence because a person is assured that he cannot be harmed without God's will.

# CHAPTER 4
# THE FIVE PILLARS

## ACTS OF WORSHIP IN ISLAM

### Concept of Ibadah (worship)

In Islam, worship consists of far more than the performance of some ritual acts of worship, such as prayers and fasting. It encompasses everything that one says, believes, or does for God's pleasure including:

❑ Rituals
❑ Beliefs
❑ Social interactions
❑ Personal acts
❑ Community service
❑ Other activities

In Arabic, the word "Ibadah" means worship as well as service. Therefore, the Islamic concept of worship, or Ibadah, means worshipping as well as serving God. It derives from obedience and slavery to God. The essence of Ibadah is the feeling of gratitude towards God. In Islam, every action performed with the intention of pleasing God, or carrying out His commands, is considered to be an act of worship or Ibadah. Acts that can be considered Ibadah include visiting a sick person, helping a stranger, forgiving someone, etc.

An important aspect of any act of worship is the intention behind it. It is the factor that determines how a deed is judged—whether it is the fulfillment of an act of worship, a particular obligation, or any routine act. Through intentions, one's daily routine can be turned into worship or Ibadah. Acts that can be converted into worship include the performance of personal and social interactions including eating, drinking, sexual relations with spouse, supporting the family emotionally and financially, etc.

## Ritual worship: The five pillars

There are five pillars of Islam and all of them are mandatory for Muslims. They are:

❑ Declaration of faith: to recite at least once during a lifetime, "There is no God but God and Muhammad[P] is His prophet"

❑ Prayers: pray five times per day

❑ Alms-giving: give charity annually, at a rate of 2.5 percent of savings

❑ Fasting: fast for one month during the month of Ramadan

❑ Hajj: visit Mecca for pilgrimage once in a lifetime, if financial and physical conditions permit

None of the five pillars can be ignored or rejected by a Muslim. They are viewed as the foundations upon which faith is built and include both faith and ritual worship. If one fails to follow any of the five pillars, it is considered to be a very serious sin in Islam.

The acts of worship are intended to achieve the following :

❑ Make the believer accept God's sovereignty

❑ Make the believer surrender to God

❑ Make the believer obey God's commands

❑ Constantly remind the believer of God

❑ Organize a believer's life, and everyday activities, around it

❑ Elevate a believer morally and spiritually

## Non-ritual worship

There are many types of activities, besides formal ritual worship, that are considered acts of worship in Islam. They can be as varied as:

❏  Seeking knowledge
❏  Social courtesy and cooperation when performed for the sake of God; acts can be as simple as greeting someone with a smile, providing encouragement, or visiting a sick person
❏  Performing normal duties
❏  Showing kindness to family members
❏  Performing deeds of righteousness

With Islam regulating every aspect of life, performing day-to-day activities according to the Islamic way ensures that the believer is performing worship all day long. The knowledge that a great reward awaits him ensures that a true believer will always be trying his best to be good, even without the incentive of worldly benefits, in every aspect of his life.

# PILLAR #1: DECLARATION OF FAITH (SHAHADAH)

## Basic declaration for accepting or reaffirming Islam

The first pillar of Islam is the declaration of faith. It is called the "Shahadah", which means witness in Arabic. The declaration, which is in Arabic, can be translated as, "There is no god but God; Muhammad[P] is the messenger of God." Recitation of the Shahadah is used as the formal means of entry into Islam.

The declaration of faith can be broken into three parts, each of which has fairly deep implications. They are:

❑ "No god" implies a rejection of polytheism—indicates that no one can share the divine attributes of God.

❑ "but God" affirms monotheism and what it implies—that God is the only one worthy of worship.

❑ "Muhammad[P] is the messenger of God" affirms the prophethood of Muhammad[P]. It implies following the teachings of Muhammad[P].

The acceptance of God and His oneness, or Tawheed, is the fundamental and central concept of Islam. The declaration of faith, when recited in sincerity, means that the person saying it:

❑ Accepts the unique position and sovereignty of God and, therefore, surrenders to Him; such a person affirms and restricts divinity to God alone.

❑ Rejects the worship of everyone, other than God, including angels, prophets, God's creations, and any human being no matter what his position, religious standing, wealth or power.

## Importance of Shahadah

There can be no entry into Islam unless a person recites the Shahadah—the declaration of faith. The first pillar is the foundation upon which everything else is based. If a person does not accept either God or Muhammad[P], through denial of a part or all of the declaration, it means he rejects Islam. The Shahadah is recited in the call to prayers, which precedes every ritual prayer, as well as in the ritual prayers. It serves as a constant reminder of God and His messenger.

When a non-Muslim recites the declaration of faith, all of his previous sins are forgiven and he starts a new life with a clean slate. For Muslims, the declaration is a commitment to a life of service in the way of God. It puts them on the path where they have to constantly worship Him and, in every aspect of their lives, make a conscientious decision to choose good over evil.

# PILLAR #2: PRAYER (SALAT)

## Requirement and objective

The second pillar of Islam is ritual prayer, which is called "Salat" in Arabic. Muslims are mandated to pray five times a day. The time required to complete these prayers, which are of different length, varies from approximately five to ten minutes. The timings for the five mandatory prayers are:

- ☐ Dawn (Fajr): to be performed between dawn and sunrise
- ☐ Noon/Early afternoon (Zohar): to be performed in the early part of the afternoon
- ☐ Mid-late afternoon (Asr): to be performed between late afternoon and sunset
- ☐ Sunset (Maghrib): to be performed from sunset till just before the Isha prayer starts
- ☐ Nightfall (Isha): preferably to be performed from the time when twilight disappears until $1/3^{rd}$ of the night has passed; however, it can be offered till dawn

A person can pray ritually more than five times a day. It is usual for Muslims to offer special ritual prayers, even though they are not mandated, for many special occasions. Special prayers are offered when a Muslim wants to thank God for some special favor or achievement, during times of adversity, when entering a mosque, other special occasions, etc.

A ritual prayer can be offered anywhere including the home, office, factory, corridor, playground, shopping center, etc. However, it is recommended that one should try to offer as many prayers as possible in a congregation, preferably in a mosque. When any ritual prayer is offered, the worshipper's face must be turned towards the direction of Mecca. However, there is no such requirement for informal, non-ritual, worship.

## Benefit of prayers

There are many features and benefits of prayers. The important ones that can be identified include:

- ❑ Increases God-consciousness and enables direct contact with God five times a day
- ❑ On the Day of Judgment, the first question required to be answered by everyone will concern the performance, or non-performance, of the mandatory prayers
- ❑ Makes a believer strive for the hereafter
- ❑ Enables a believer to show devotion and obedience to God
- ❑ Strengthens fear and love of God
- ❑ Reminds the believer of God and His commands
- ❑ Provides opportunity to thank God for His blessings, ask for forgiveness and request His guidance
- ❑ Becomes the distinctive characteristic of a believer
- ❑ Is the practical manifestation of faith
- ❑ Makes a believer disciplined
- ❑ Uplifts morally and spiritually
- ❑ Enhances community feelings due to congregational prayers
- ❑ Helps avoid bad deeds through constant reminders

## Prerequisites for prayers

There are a few prerequisites that need to be met before a ritual prayer can be offered. They include:

❑ Ablution (called Wudu in Arabic): includes mandatory washing of face, hands, and feet as well as wiping the head; wiping neck and ears, as well as rinsing the mouth, are recommended

❑ Full ablution: if someone has had intercourse, or a woman's menstruation has just ended, a bath is mandated prior to prayers

❑ Chosen spot for offering the prayer, as well as prayer rug, should be clean

❑ Shoes must be taken off if they are unclean

❑ Making an informal intention to offer the prayer

❑ The face is to be turned towards the direction of Kaaba (Mecca); it should be noted that God, and not the Kaaba, is the object of worship

## How a prayer is performed

An informal, non-ritual, act of worship can be performed at any time and anywhere. Such worship requires no specific actions to be performed or words to be recited. Recitation, if any, can be performed silently or loudly. It is also not necessary to face Mecca for informal worship. Such worship, or informal prayer, can be performed as many times as one desires during the day or night.

The formal prayers, which are required to be memorized and recited in Arabic, are performed as per a specific procedure. However, there are some minor variations, both in actions and in the prayer recitation, among various Islamic sects. The most commonly followed prayer procedure involves the following sequence of steps:

1. Stand up; face the direction of Mecca, and make an intention to offer the prayer.

2. Raise both hands to the ear level or the shoulder and say "God is the Greatest."

3. Fold the arms over the chest, with the right over the left.

4. Recite, "Praise and glory be to you O God. Blessed be Your Name, exalted be Your Majesty and Glory. There is no God but You."
5. Recite, "I seek God's shelter from Satan, the condemned."
6. Recite, " In the Name of God, the Beneficent, the Merciful."
7. Recite the opening chapter of the Koran (al-Fatiha).
8. Recite any other chapter, usually a small one, or a few verses from the Koran.
9. Say "God is the Greatest" while bending over and placing the palms on the knees.
10. While still bent over, say "Glorified is my Lord, the Great!" three times.
11. Stand up and say, "Allah listens to him who praises Him" and "Our Lord! Praise be for You only."
12. Say "God is the Greatest."
13. Prostrate to the ground so that the forehead, palms, nose, knees, and toes touch it.
14. Say "Glory to God, the Exalted" three times.
15. Say "God is the Greatest" while changing from the prostrate position to a sitting position.
16. Say "God is the Greatest" while changing from the sitting position to the prostrate position.
17. Again, say "Glory to God, the Exalted" three times.
18. While saying "God is the Greatest," stand upright.
19. Fold the arms over the chest, with the right over the left.
20. Repeat Steps 7 through 17.
21. Sit down in a kneeling position, with the lower part of the legs touching the ground.
22. Recite "Tashahud" and "Salat Ala An-Nabi" which are verses containing supplications and prayers (see next section for their translation).
23. Turn the face to the right and say, " Peace and mercy of God be on you."
24. Turn the face to the left and say, "Peace and mercy of God be on you."

In the procedure just explained, the worshipper completed two "rakat" or units. Each rakat involved touching the forehead to the ground two times. All the formal prayers comprise either two, three or four rakats, which means bowing four, six or eight times respectively. The mandatory component of the dawn prayer comprises two rakats, both the afternoon prayers four rakats, sunset prayer three rakats, and nightfall prayer four rakats.

## Examples of verses recited during ritual prayers

### al-Fatiha

This is the opening chapter of the Koran, which is recited in every ritual prayer. The following is its translation:
In the name of Allah, the beneficent, the merciful
Praise be to Allah, Lord of the Worlds
The beneficent, the merciful
Master of the Day of Judgment
Thee do we worship, and Thine aid we seek
Show us the straight path
The path of those whom Thou hast favored
Not the (path) of those who earn Thine anger nor of those who go astray

### Tashahud

All our oral, physical, and monetary ways of worship are only for God
Peace, mercy and blessing of God be on you, O prophet
May peace be upon us and on the devout slaves of God
I bear witness that there is no god but God
I bear witness that Muhammad[P] is His slave and messenger."

### Salat Ala an-Nabi

O God! Send your mercy on Muhammad[P]
And his posterity
As you sent your mercy on Abraham
And his posterity
You are the most praised, the most glorious
O God! Send your blessings on Muhammad[P]
And his posterity
As you have blessed Abraham
And his posterity
You are the most praised, the most glorious

After completion of a ritual formal prayer in Arabic, worshippers typically offer supplications, usually in their own language. The post-prayer dialogue with God can cover a wide range of subjects including request for help, acknowledgement of his favors, gratitude, forgiveness, wishes, desires, etc.

## Congregational prayers

The ritual Friday afternoon prayer is a mandatory congregational prayer. It is preceded by a short sermon which can be delivered by any knowledgeable Muslim, in any language though Arabic is recommended. The sermon can address any topic, with the most popular subjects being religion, current events, politics, community affairs, and social issues. Prayers are usually led by the most knowledgeable, or older and pious, person in the congregation. The basic requirement for leading the prayer is that the leader must have memorized the few Arabic verses that need to be recited during the performance of the formal prayer.

Muslims are encouraged to offer their daily ritual prayers in a congregation, whenever possible. A congregational prayer can be performed with as few as two worshippers. Such a prayer can be offered, just like any other prayer, at home or elsewhere. However, if it is offered in a mosque, it is awarded the highest reward.

In a congregation prayer, all the worshippers stand next to each other in straight lines. The leader recites the prayer loudly and the congregation follows him as he performs various actions like bowing, kneeling, and prostrating. A benefit of the congregational prayer is that it fosters a sense of equality because all the worshippers have to stand and prostrate together, irrespective of whether they are farmers, workers, Sheiks, ministers, millionaires or paupers. A king may pray in the line behind a janitor. At prayer time, all classes vanish and everyone is reminded of God—their object of worship.

## Call to prayer

In Muslim communities, there is a call to prayer five times a day corresponding to the prayer times. The call to prayer consists of the following verses:

God is the greatest; God is the greatest
God is the greatest; God is the greatest
I bear witness that there is no god except God
I bear witness that there is no god except God
I bear witness that Muhammad[P] is the messenger of God
I bear witness that Muhammad[P] is the messenger of God
Come to prayer; Come to prayer
Come to success; Come to success
God is the greatest; God is the greatest
There is no god except God

## Role of imams in prayer

Mainstream orthodox Islam does not recognize formal priesthood and, hence, there exists no formal, hierarchical, or religious authority in Muslim societies. However, within the Shia sect, which constitutes about ten percent of the Muslim population, there is a well-organized formal religious hierarchy. Nowadays, in many Muslim communities, mosques retain paid imams, or prayer leaders, who lead the five daily congregational prayers. Some religious scholars with extensive education in theology, called "Ulema", also lead prayers and religious functions. They are highly respected but they have no authority to change any law or Islamic tradition. They are viewed as spiritual teachers who provide Islamic education and guidance in the day-to-day life of the Muslim community.

# PILLAR #3: ALMS-GIVING (ZAKAT)

## Requirement and objective

The third pillar of Islam is mandatory alms-giving. In Arabic, it is called zakat, which means purification. In this case, the reference is to the purification of wealth from greed, miserliness, and selfishness. According to Islam, everything in this world belongs to God and any wealth held by man is in trust as a temporary custodian. A part of the wealth accumulated by an individual belongs to other people and must be distributed to them. If the trust is not discharged, the wealth becomes impure and unclean.

In practical terms, zakat is a simple wealth tax that is required to be paid by individuals who meet certain criteria. Failure to pay zakat is considered a serious sin in Islam. Its importance can be gauged from the fact that it is mentioned more than 30 times in the Koran, usually in conjunction with prayers.

Zakat is levied on the net wealth that a person has accumulated. To estimate the zakat due, all the assets are first valued and totaled. Assets to be totaled include cash, investments, inventory, etc. From the total assets value (minus a few exemptions that are allowed), all debts and liabilities are subtracted. The remainder is subject to zakat at a flat 2.5 percent rate. If liabilities exceed assets, no zakat is due.

It should be noted that a person's residence as well as his personal car are exempt from zakat. Therefore, they are not to be included in the assets to be used in the zakat calculations. There is some disagreement among the various Islamic schools of thought about the value of jewelry to be included in the zakat calculations. Some consider jewelry to be an exempt item.

## Benefits of zakat

The expected benefits from paying zakat are:
- Brings the believer closer to God through this act of worship
- Earns rewards for the giver who will be compensated in the hereafter
- Shows devotion to God by following His command
- Redistributes wealth without hurting those who have accumulated wealth
- Makes the rich provide for the poor and needy; helps them get rid of any greed and selfishness that they may have
- Makes people think about the disadvantaged members of society and contributes to social stability
- Makes people acquire qualities like sympathy, mercy, and benevolence

## When and how much Zakat needs to be distributed

Zakat is due once a year and every individual can choose his own time to pay it. Most Muslims prefer to pay during the holy month of Ramadan, though that is not a requirement. The recipient of zakat must meet certain eligibility requirements. It is the responsibility of the donor, if he chooses to pay zakat directly to a needy person rather than through some organization, to determine the recipient's eligibility for zakat. The donor must also ensure that the zakat recipient is not taunted or made to lose self-respect.

During the earlier periods of Islamic rule, the state used to collect zakat and deposit it in a zakat fund, like the social security trust fund, which was used to help support the poor and needy. In the modern world, few Islamic governments collect zakat. Therefore, with some exceptions, zakat distribution has become a personal responsibility. Typically, zakat donations are made to individuals and various collection centers such as mosques, Islamic centers, and social organizations.

## Optional alms-giving

The minimum zakat obligation is 2.5 percent. However, an individual can contribute more than that amount. Besides the mandatory zakat, Islam encourages the giving of voluntary charity. Such charity, known as "Sadaqa", can be paid in kind or cash and can be distributed at any time.

# PILLAR #4: FASTING (SAWM)

## Requirement and objective

The fourth pillar of Islam is fasting during the month of Ramadan, which is the ninth month of the Islamic calendar. In Arabic, it is called "Sawm."

Ramadan is considered a holy month by Muslims for two reasons. Firstly, the Koran was first revealed to Muhammad[P] in Ramadan. Secondly, it has been designated as the month of fasting.

Fasting is mandatory for all Muslims, who are able-bodied adults in good health, for the full month of Ramadan. Children are expected to begin fasting when they attain puberty. Fasting is more than a physical exercise. It is a form of worship and a fasting Muslim, throughout the day, remembers God for whom the fast is undertaken. Fasting teaches self-control and patience. Like prayer, it is a way for Muslims to turn to God in sincere worship.

The objectives of Ramadan fasting are:
❑   Worship God and obey His command
❑   Seek closeness to God
❑   Show gratitude to God
❑   Perform self-purification
❑   Learn self-restraint and control material desires
❑   Gain piety
❑   Remember the needy

## What fasting involves

Fasting involves complete abstinence, from dawn till sunset, from eating or drinking. However, routine day-to-day activities must continue to be conducted while fasting. Sexual intercourse is prohibited so long as a fast is in effect. There is no restriction on eating and drinking from sunset to the following dawn. On the spiritual side, a fasting person must abstain from lying, anger, fighting or quarreling, gossiping, and other negative activities that Islam has prohibited.

Typically, a fast is started by having a heavy meal at dawn. The fast is ended at sunset, usually by eating a few dates and having a light snack, which is followed by the sunset prayer. After the prayer, a heavy meal is enjoyed which is followed by snacks till bed time. Usually, the breaking of a fast is converted into a social event. Friends and family members get together and collectively break the fast.

## Benefits of fasting

There are many benefits of fasting including:
- Being rewarded on the Day of Judgment
- Being rewarded with God's love because He loves those who fast
- Increases awareness of God
- Reminds believers of dependence upon and relationship to God
- Improves spirituality
- Achieves inner purification
- Provides a benchmark, once a year, against which Muslims can compare themselves
- Elevates moral standards
- Improves physical and spiritual health
- Makes everyone aware of what hungry people undergo
- Improves social consciousness and care for others
- Improves discipline and self-restraint
- Forces one to be patient and reflective

## Fasting exemptions

While fasting is mandatory, there are many exemptions that take into consideration various constraints and limitations of people that can be expected in any society. For example, old and sick people, pregnant and nursing women, menstruating women, and travelers are exempted from fasting. If physically able to do so, they are required to make up the missed fasts later on during the year. If unable to fast, a Muslim has to feed at least one poor person for each missed fast.

## Fasting calendar

The Islamic lunar-based calendar is shorter than the solar calendar by 11 days. Therefore, Ramadan starts earlier each year by 11 days, which means that it falls in every season over an extended period of many years. A believer, over his life span, will see Ramadan in the summer, when days are long and hot, as well as during winter when days are short and cold. The typical duration of a fast is 10-16 hours which corresponds to the length of the day at a particular location.

## Difficulty in fasting

The general impression, among those who have not experienced it, is that fasting is very difficult physically. While fasting does test a person due to self-inflicted hunger, the physical test is easier than the non-physical test of controlling anger, being patient, ignoring aggravations, and avoiding other emotions and acts that displease God. For example, if the normal tendency of a person is to retaliate immediately, it is easier for such a person to be hungry than to avoid retaliation—which is expected of him during Ramadan.

## Penalty for breaking a fast

A fast can be broken if there is danger to one's health. If a fast is broken unintentionally, or due to a medical condition, it can be made up later. If one breaks a fast intentionally, the penalty imposed is fasting for 60 continuous days. However, in case one is unable to fast continuously for 60 days, the penalty is feeding 60 needy people or donating to charity an amount equal to the cost of feeding 60 people.

## Extra activities during Ramadan

In addition to being a challenging month, Ramadan is also a very busy period for Muslims. During the month of Ramadan, there are additional religious as well as social activities that keep everyone quite busy. The following are some activities that characterize Ramadan:

❑ Muslims are encouraged to:
   o   Read the whole Koran from cover to cover
   o   Show more generosity and give extra charity
❑ Special congregational prayers of 8 or 20 rakats (units), called Taraweeh, are held in mosques after the nightfall prayers
❑ During the course of the month, a complete Koran is recited in the Taraweeh prayers
❑ On Lailat al-Qadr, which is the anniversary of the first revelation of the Koran, Muslims spend the night in worship at home or in a mosque

## Celebrating the end of Ramadan

Eid al-Fitr is the day of celebration which follows the last day of Ramadan. Following a congregational prayer, Muslims visit friends and relatives. Friends and family members are greeted by a hug. People wear new clothes and children are given cash or gifts by their parents and relatives. On this day, Zakat al-Fitr, a type of donation, is given to the poor. After a month of self-control, people enjoy assorted foods and the mood is very festive. Muslim countries mark this day as an official holiday.

## Non-Ramadan fasting

There are a number of other days, in non-Ramadan months, that are recommended for optional fasting. They include the first six days of the month of Shawwal, which follows Ramadan, as well as the 9$^{th}$ and 10$^{th}$ of Muharram. An optional fast can be kept on any day of the year, except on the two main festival days: Eid al-Fitr and Eid al-Adha.

# PILLAR #5: PILGRIMAGE TO MECCA (HAJJ)

## Requirement and objective

The fifth pillar of Islam is Hajj—the once in a lifetime pilgrimage to Mecca. Hajj falls in Dhu al-Hijjah, the 12$^{th}$ month of the Islamic calendar, and is mandatory only for those who can afford it and are physically able to perform it. Over two million Muslims from all over the world perform Hajj each year.

The purpose of the Hajj pilgrimage, which consists of a number of rituals and acts of worship, is to worship and please God. Its culmination is marked by commemorating the attempt by Prophet Abraham to sacrifice his son, Ishmael, when he was ordered to do so by God in order to test his loyalty and obedience.

## Benefits of Hajj

The benefits that Muslims hope to achieve from Hajj include the following:
- Ability to respond to God's commands
- Opportunity to thank God for His grace and the favors He has bestowed
- Purification—be cleansed of sins and start a new life
- Patience, endurance, self-restraint, and piety
- Breaking down of racial, economic, and social barriers
- Meeting Muslims from all over the world and experiencing brotherhood

# What performing the Hajj involves

## *Dress code*

Hajj has to be performed in a state of "Ihram", which is achieved by wearing a special type of dress. All male pilgrims wear two unsown white garments, which sweep away all distinctions of background, status, wealth, and culture. Women usually wear a modest white dress, though no specific clothing has been prescribed for them. During the state of Ihram, when the white pilgrim clothes are worn, a pilgrim cannot kill an insect or animal, cut any body hair, engage in a sexual act, commit violence, or become angry.

## *Rituals and activities*

The rituals associated with Hajj can be traced back to Prophet Abraham. They start on the 8th day of Dhu al-Hijjah and include:

- ❑ Tawaf, which involves circling the Kaaba seven times in a counter-clockwise manner.
- ❑ Touching the black stone of the Kaaba.
- ❑ Drinking water from the Zam Zam spring.
- ❑ Sa'i: walking briskly between Safa and Marwa, two small hills near the Kaaba, seven times to retrace the path Hagar took when searching for water for her son Ishmael.
- ❑ Camping at Mina when the Hajj begins formally on 8th Dhu al-Hijjah. Pilgrims stay at Mina extends from dawn on 8th Dhu al-Hijjah to after dawn on 9th Dhu al-Hijjah (when they proceed to Arafat).
- ❑ Pilgrims assemble at Arafat, a large empty plain outside Mecca, on 9th Dhu al-Hijjah. At this site, there is supplication to God and pilgrims pray for mercy and forgiveness. They listen to a sermon, during the afternoon prayers, in commemoration of the final pilgrimage by Muhammad[P] who delivered his farewell sermon from Arafat.

❑ Stay at Arafat on 9$^{th}$ Dhu al-Hijjah from after dawn to slightly after sunset (when pilgrims proceed to Muzdalfa).

❑ Stay at Muzdalfa from after sunset on 9$^{th}$ Dhu al-Hijjah to after dawn on 10$^{th}$ Dhu al-Hijjah.

❑ Proceed to Mina and throw 7 pebbles at Jamrat-ul-Aqaba—symbols of Satan who attempted to make Abraham disobey God's command.

❑ Sacrifice an animal, to commemorate Abraham's attempt to sacrifice his son, on 10$^{th}$ Dhu al-Hijjah—which is the Eid al-Adha festival day.

❑ Male pilgrims shave their head and change into everyday clothes.

❑ Proceed to Mecca and perform the Tawaf; this particular Tawaf is known as Tawaf al-Ifadah.

❑ Return to Mina, where the stay extends from 11-13$^{th}$ Dhu al-Hijjah, and stone three pillars—symbols of Satan.

❑ Return to Mecca to perform the farewell Tawaf—known as Tawaf al-Widaa.

Among the listed rituals, the only mandatory requirements of Hajj are:

❑ Presence at Arafat on 9$^{th}$ Dhu al-Hijjah

❑ Performing Tawaf al-Ifadah

Many pilgrims also visit Muhammad$^{P}$'s grave in Medina either before or after Hajj.

## Eid al-Adha and the sacrifice

The Eid al-Adha festival marks the end of Hajj. On that day, the 10$^{th}$ of Dhu al-Hijjah, which is a public holiday in Muslim countries, a congregational prayer is offered in the morning. Following the prayer, an animal is sacrificed to commemorate Abraham's readiness to obey God's command and sacrifice his son. On Eid al-Adha, in Muslim communities throughout the world, an animal is sacrificed and its meat distributed to relatives, neighbors, and the needy. The sacrifice, which can be performed by a

Muslim himself or someone else on his behalf, is an obligation for those able to afford it financially. On Eid al-Adha, children are given cash or gifts and people wear new clothes.

# CHAPTER 5
# ISLAMIC CONCEPT OF GOD

## FUNDAMENTAL CONCEPTS

### Monotheism: Belief in one God

The most important concept in Islam is monotheism, or Tawheed, which is based upon the fundamental belief that there is only one God and that He has no partners or equals. According to Islam, if a person compromises that concept in any way, none of his acts of worship will be accepted by God.

Muslims are required to acknowledge, as part of their basic beliefs, that God alone must be worshipped. Worshipping anything else is a rejection of God. Also required from them is confirmation of His other names and attributes, which are listed in a subsequent section.

### Monotheism: Three perspectives

The belief in monotheism has three distinct aspects. They are
❑   Oneness of God
❑   Worship of only one God
❑   Uniqueness in the names and attributes of God

## Oneness of God

Muslims believe that God is one and only one. Their primary beliefs relating to the oneness of God include the following:

❑ God created everything and controls everything in the universe
❑ Everything happens according to His will
❑ God determines when life starts and ends
❑ God shares no power with any partners or equals
❑ Only God knows the future
❑ God can be reached directly; He does not require any intermediaries for humans to reach Him
❑ God neither begets nor is He begotten; He created Adam without parents and Jesus without a father

## Worship of only one God

Islam teaches that only God must be worshipped, which is the purpose of man's creation. Muslims are taught to worship only the Creator and not His creations—the message delivered by every prophet sent by God. The objective of every prophet, always, was to lead his people back to monotheism from which they had deviated over time.

The concept of worshipping God is unique in Islam. It is not limited to ritual acts of worship. Instead, it encompasses all of life's activities that are carried out with the objective of pleasing God.

## Uniqueness in the names and attributes of God

Islam teaches that God has very unique attributes that are not shared by anyone else. For example:

❑ He is perfect and unique
❑ He is the creator of everything
❑ He has no beginning or end and lives forever

❑   He never gets tired
❑   He is the sustainer and protector of everything
❑   He has unlimited knowledge about everything that has happened and
    what will happen

## Shirk: The unpardonable sin

Islam makes a very clear distinction between God and His creations. It
teaches that none of God's creations must be worshipped either directly or
indirectly. Any failure to differentiate between the Creator and His creations is considered a very serious sin. The most serious and unpardonable
sin in Islam is *Shirk*, which refers to the worship of any creation and associating partners with God. It includes:
❑   Polytheism
❑   Concept of Trinity


# QUALITIES, ATTRIBUTES AND EXPECTATIONS

## Qualities and characteristics

In addition to the basic and fundamental Islamic beliefs about God, there
are other aspects that define what He means to Muslims. These include,
but are not limited to, the following qualities and characteristics of God:
❑   He is all-powerful
❑   He is absolutely just and merciful
❑   He is compassionate and forgiving
❑   He is most gracious
❑   He is supreme and sovereign
❑   He is all-seeing and all-hearing
❑   He has no defects
❑   He is the true guide

❑ He is the provider
❑ He is free from weariness and weakness
❑ He is wise and knows what is best for us
❑ He loves those who worship Him
❑ He likes good deeds and dislikes what He has prohibited
❑ He knows everything that we think and feel
❑ He sent His prophets including the last one, Muhammad[P]
❑ He revealed the scriptures including the Koran
❑ On the Day of Judgment, everyone will have to answer to Him

## God's 99 attributes

Muslims believe that God has 99 names and attributes, which are listed below along with their translated meanings in parenthesis. It should be realized that these are close, but not always equal, translations from Arabic which is a very rich language:

1. Allah (God)
2. Al-Rahman (The Compassionate, The Beneficent, The Gracious)
3. Al-Rahim (The Merciful)
4. Al-Malik (The King)
5. Al-Quddus (The Most Holy)
6. Al-Salam (The Source of Peace)
7. Al-Mumin (Guardian of Faith)
8. Al-Muhaymin (The Protector)
9. Al-Aziz (The Mighty)
10. Al-Jabbar (The Compeller)
11. Al-Mutakabbir (The Majestic)
12. Al-Khaliq (The Creator)
13. Al-Bari (The Maker)
14. Al-Musawwir (The Bestower of Form, The Shaper)
15. Al-Ghaffar (The Forgiver)
16. Al-Qahhar (The Subduer)
17. Al-Wahhab (The Bestower)
18. Al-Razzaq (The Provider, The Sustainer)
19. Al-Fattah (The Opener, The Judge)

20. Al-Alim (The All-Knowing
21. Al-Qabid (The Withholder)
22. Al-Basit (The Expander)
23. Al-Khafid (The Abaser)
24. Al-Rafi (The Exalter)
25. Al-Mu'izz
    (The Bestower of Honor)
26. Al-Mudhill (The Humiliator)
27. Al-Sami (The All-Hearing)
28. Al-Basir (The All-Seeing)
29. Al-Hakam (The Judge)
30. Al-Adl
    (The Just, The Equitable)
31. Al-Latif
    (The Gentle, The Subtle One)
32. Al-Khabir (The All-Aware)
33. Al-Halim (The Forbearing)
34. Al-Azim (The Great One)
35. Al-Ghafoor (The Forgiving)
36. Ash-Shakoor
    (The Appreciative)
37. Al-Aliyy (The Most High)
38. Al-Kabir (The Great)
39. Al-Hafiz (The Preserver)
40. Al-Muqit (The Sustainer)
41. Al-Hasib (The Reckoner)
42. Al-Jalil
    (The Majestic, The Sublime)
43. Al-Karim (The Generous)
44. Al-Raqib (The Watchful)
45. Al-Mujib (The Responsive)

46. Al-Wasi
    (The All-Encompassing,
    The All-Embracing)
47. Al-Hakim (The Wise)
48. Al-Wadud (The Loving)
49. Al-Majid (The Glorious)
50. Al-Baith (The Resurrector)
51. Al-Shahid (The Witness)
52. Al-Haqq (The Truth)
53. Al-Wakil (The Trustee)
54. Al-Qawiyy (The Strong)
55. Al-Matin (The Firm)
56. Al-Waliyy (The Protector)
57. Al-Hamid (The Praiseworthy)
58. Al-Muhsi (The Reckoner)
59. Al-Mubdi (The Originator)
60. Al-Muid (The Restorer)
61. Al-Muhyi (The Giver of Life)
62. Al-Mumit (The Taker of Life)
63. Al-Hayy (The Ever-Living)
64. Al-Qayyum
    (The Self-Existing)
65. Al-Wajid
    (The Perceiver, The Finder)
66. Al-Majid (The Glorious)
67. Al-Wahid (The One)
68. Al-Samad
    (The Eternally Besought)
69. Al-Qadir
    (The Omnipotent, The Able)
70. Al-Muqtadir (The Powerful)

71. Al-Muqaddim (The Expeditor)
72. Al-Mu'akhkhir (The Delayer)
73. Al-Awwal (The First)
74. Al-Akhir (The Last)
75. Al-Zahir (The Manifest)
76. Al-Batin (The Hidden)
77. Al-Wali (The Governor)
78. Al-Muta'ali (The Most Exalted)
79. Al-Barr (The Source of All Goodness)
80. Al-Tawwab (The Acceptor of Repentance)
81. Al-Afuww (The Pardoner)
82. Al-Muntaqim (The Avenger)
83. Al-Rauf (The Clement)
84. Malik ul-Mulk (The Owner of the Kingdom)
85. Dhul Jalal wal-Ikram (The Lord of Majesty and Bounty)
86. Al-Muqsit (The Equitable)
87. Al-Jami (The Gatherer)
88. Al-Ghaniyy (The Self-Sufficient)
89. Al-Mughni (The Enricher)
90. Al-Mani (The Preventer)
91. Al-Nafi (The Benefiter)
92. Al-Darr (The Afflicter)
93. Al-Noor (The Light)
94. Al-Hadi (The Guide)
95. Al-Badi (The Incomparable)
96. Al-Baqi (The Everlasting)
97. Al-Warith (The Ultimate Inheritor)
98. Al-Rashid (The Guide)
99. Al-Sabur (The Patient One)

A Muslim is expected to have firm beliefs about God and all His attributes. He cannot believe in some attributes while disbelieving others.

## What God expects from man

According to Islam, God created man so that he may worship Him. He generously bestowed many favors on mankind but does not need anything in return because He is independent and has no needs. However, what He requires is for believers to recognize His unique and exalted position, worship Him, obey His commands without question, and strive to lead a life that will ensure a place in heaven for them. He wants man to perform as many activities as possible with the pleasure of God in mind. By doing what is expected of him, man can expect to be fully rewarded in the hereafter.

## What to expect from God

The Islamic view of God is that He is very just. Muslims are taught that they should expect to be rewarded or punished, depending on how they live their lives. For example:

❑ Sinners and evil doers will be punished
❑ Virtuous people will be rewarded with favors
❑ Oppressors will be punished
❑ Creation worshippers will not be forgiven

Muslims are also taught that they can expect pardon and forgiveness even for the most serious sins, if they are sincerely regretful and repentant, because God is forgiving. Other expectations from God include:

❑ Listening to prayers
❑ Providing help
❑ Love for those who love Him

# CONCEPT OF DIRECT RELATIONSHIP

## Man has a direct relationship with God

Islam teaches that every human being has a direct one-on-one relationship with God. In order to communicate with Him, no intermediary is required. Therefore, one can pray to God anytime and anywhere. It is this concept that eliminates the need for clergy or priesthood for mainstream Muslims.

## Role of clergy and scholars

In mainstream Islam, as represented by the Sunni sect, the concept of priesthood or clergy and ordainment does not exist because there is no need or requirement for someone to act as an intermediary between an individual Muslim and God.

Some knowledgeable Islamic experts, who have formal Islamic education and training, often serve as leaders of their community. They lead congregational prayers and issue rulings on various religious and social issues. However, they have no formal position sanctioned by Islam. An "Alim" is an Islamic scholar who has thoroughly studied the Koran, the teachings of Muhammad[P], as well as associated Islamic literature. Such scholars also have formal religious degrees from Islamic institutions and Universities.

In practically every orthodox Muslim community, there is an imam—a community religious leader. The responsibilities of imams can vary tremendously. In small communities, especially in rural areas, they are responsible for leading congregational prayers, teaching Islam and Koran recitation, and performing marriage ceremonies. Their role and duties are, to a large extent, determined by their local community. In some communities, especially in more educated communities, they have additional responsibilities such as teaching Islam and Arabic, Islamic interpretation of social and other issues, issuing religious opinions (fatwa), ensuring that politicians and local leaders do not violate Islamic principles, etc.

The mainstream imams, who follow orthodox Islam and belong to the Sunni sect, should not be confused with the Shia imams, who play a completely different role for their followers, which is explained in the next section.

Within Muslim communities, there is another group of scholars known as "Haafiz." Typically, they are the products of Islamic seminaries where they obtain Islamic education and memorize the Koran from cover-to-cover. Since memorizing the Koran has high rewards associated with it, many ordinary Muslims, even outside such seminaries, memorize the Koran and become Haafiz. The ranks of the Haafiz have included children, doctors, engineers, businessmen, as well as people from all walks of life.

## Imams and ayatollahs

In the Shia sect of Islam, there exists a well structured religious hierarchy headed by imams and ayatollahs. The Shia sect structure and power hierarchy is somewhat similar to the Catholic Church. At the highest level in their hierarchy are the imams, who are the direct descendants of Muhammad[P]. Shias believe that there have been 12 imams, starting with Muhammad[P]'s son-in-law Ali ibn Abu Talib, who have had supreme religious authority. In the absence of an imam, the authority is discharged by the ayatollahs, who are highly learned Shia scholars.

The Shias believe that while a prophet is a messenger of God, an imam is Prophet Muhammad[P]'s messenger. The difference is that while a prophet receives a revelation from God, an imam receives commands from the prophet through a special blessing. Imams are viewed as having Pope-like infallibility.

# CHAPTER 6
# KORAN, SUNNAH, SHARIA, AND GOVERNMENT

## KORAN

### What is the Koran

The Koran, which means recitation, is the word of God that was revealed in Arabic to Muhammad[P] through Angel Gabriel. The Koranic revelations which started in Mecca, and continued in Medina, were revealed from 610 through 632. The Koran is characterized by a unique style that makes it highly readable and easy to memorize. Another defining characteristic is that it has remained completely immune to any alterations in nearly 14 centuries, as promised by God in the Koranic verse, "We have, without doubt, sent down the Message; and We will assuredly guard it (from corruption) (15:9)."

The Koran has been translated into every major language. Among the English translations, the most popular ones are by Abdullah Yusuf Ali, Muhammad Taqi-ud-Din al-Hilali and Muhammad Muhsin, and Muhammad Marmaduke Pickthall. Syed Abu-Ala' Maududi's *The Meaning of the Quran,* is one of the best translations that includes a detailed commentary.

## Importance of the Koran

The Koran is the primary source of Islamic teachings. It contains God's commands, specifies Islamic beliefs, how Muslims should practice their faith, as well as Islamic laws and regulations. It is the guide that teaches Muslims how to live their lives in accordance with God's commandments and wishes. It makes mankind understand its role in this world.

## What the Koran is about

The Koran covers a wide range of subjects including spiritual, moral, social as well as day-to-day issues. The following is a partial list of the topics that are addressed in the Koran:

❑ Oneness of God and His other attributes
❑ Relationship between God and man
❑ Purpose of man's existence
❑ God's commandments
❑ Life in the hereafter
❑ Rewards and punishments
❑ Acts of worship
❑ Prophethood
❑ Moral values
❑ History
❑ Social life and family issues
❑ Inheritance
❑ Duties and responsibilities
❑ Virtues, vices, and ethical codes
❑ Conduct and interaction
❑ Crimes and punishment
❑ Economics

## How to understand the Koran

In order to properly understand the contents of the Koran, it is imperative that the background and historical context of the Koranic revelations be appreciated. Many of the verses in the Koran were revealed to provide guidance, advice, and comfort to Muhammad[P] and his followers. Such verses had direct relevance to the situation that the embattled or persecuted Muslims were encountering at that time. Therefore, one needs to be aware of the circumstances existing at the time a particular verse or chapter was revealed. Hence, it is always advisable, especially for beginners, to study the Koran that is accompanied by a detailed commentary.

Another point to keep in mind is that the Koran was revealed in Arabic—a very rich language. It is very easy to misinterpret the meaning of a word or verse because, in many cases, there is no equivalent word(s) in English or other languages. Ideally, the Koran should be studied in Arabic and, if that is not possible, then one should use a translation that is accompanied by a commentary.

## How the Koran was compiled

The Koran was revealed piecemeal over a lengthy period of more than two decades. Muhammad[P] received the first revelation in the cave of Hira, at the Mountain of Light (Jabal e-Noor) located outside the city of Mecca. Muhammad[P] and his companions, of whom there were thousands, memorized the Koranic verses as soon they were revealed. Scribes also recorded them in writing on palm leaves, parchment, animal skins, etc. Subsequently, such writings were cross-checked and verified by Muhammad[P] himself. The writing of the Koran was completed, though not compiled, by the time Muhammad[P] died.

After Muhammad[P]'s death, many Muslims who had memorized the Koran died in the battle of Yamama during the caliphate of Abu Bakr. Their loss triggered the fear that the Koran might be corrupted in the future just like the other scriptures. Therefore, Abu Bakr ordered the compilation of the Koran using both sources: written and living—from those who had memorized it. After its compilation, he took custody of the compiled Koran. Later on, the third caliph, Uthman, made many copies and distributed them.

## Koran's organization

The Koran consists of 114 chapters, known as surahs, and contains more than six thousand verses. It is divided into 30 equal parts. The chapters, which are not arranged in the order in which they were revealed, are organized according to Muhammad[P]'s instructions. The surahs are arranged with the longest chapter first and the shortest ones at the end. The longest chapter, al-Baqarah, consists of 286 verses while the shortest chapter, al-Kawthar, consists of only three verses. Typically, the place of revelation, Mecca or Medina, is indicated at the beginning of each chapter.

## Withstanding the test of time

Despite the passage of nearly 14 centuries since the Koran was revealed, it has remained completely intact and unblemished by any changes to the original text. This contrasts with the other scriptures which were edited over the centuries and, consequently, lost their authenticity.

According to the Koran, God has promised to maintain the authenticity of the Koran. Consequently, it has been able to retain its original purity and content. The belief among Muslims is that God undertook that task because He sent Muhammad[P] as the last prophet and, consequently, wanted the last scripture to remain free from blemishes. Memorizing the

Koran is considered to be a deed that will be rewarded very highly in the hereafter. Consequently, there are literally tens of thousands of Muslims, perhaps even more, who have memorized the Koran which helps to insulate it from changes creeping in.

# TEACHINGS OF THE PROPHET: SUNNAH

## What is the Sunnah

The term Sunnah literally means "way." It implies paving the way so that, later on, it becomes a way for others. In Islam, Sunnah refers to the actions, sayings, and approvals of Muhammad[P]. It is also referred to as the Hadith. The sayings and actions of Muhammad[P] were meticulously preserved and recorded. For Muslims, it is required that they follow the Sunnah, whose importance is second only to the teachings of the Koran.

## Role of the Sunnah

In the Koran, God has commanded Muslims, many times, that they should follow Muhammad[P]. According to the Koran, "Indeed in the messenger of Allah you have a good example to follow, for him who hopes for (the meeting with) Allah and the Last Day, and remembers Allah much (33:21)." It also equates obedience of the messenger with obedience of God, as is indicated in the verse, "He who obeys the messenger, obeys Allah (4:80)."

Muslims are expected to follow the example set by Muhammad[P] in his daily life. Anything that he did or say during his lifetime, and can be implemented in one's daily life, is expected to be emulated by Muslims because he is their recognized guide and role model. For example, while only two rakats, or units, are mandated for the dawn prayers, Muslims pray four rakats because Muhammad[P] used to pray the additional two rakats. Similarly, when Muhammad[P] used to put on his shoes, he always put on the right shoe first. Hence, when putting on his shoes, a Muslim will put on the right shoe first and then the left shoe.

The implementation of the Sunnah pertaining to worship acts such as prayers and fasting, called Sunnah Ibadiya, are considered more important compared to habits and routine acts. The Sunnah is complimentary with the Koran. At times, it clarifies the Koran or provides more details. Together, the Koran and Sunnah provide the basis for Sharia, or Islamic Law, which encompasses all aspects of an individual Muslim's life as well as issues of state and government.

## Koran's elevated status compared to the Sunnah

The Koran is the word of God while the Sunnah are the sayings, actions, and traditions of Muhammad[P]. Muslims hold Muhammad[P] in the highest regard. However, they recognize that he was a human being and cannot be equated to God. Consequently, they recognize the Koran as the highest source of Islamic Law and commands. The Koran as the primary source gets precedence over the Sunnah, which is the secondary source, in every respect. The secondary source cannot be in any contradiction with the primary source. If there is any inconsistency, which should not occur with a genuine Sunnah, then the Koran prevails.

## Verification of Hadith

Some time after Muhammad[P]'s death, a number of scholars recorded and complied the Hadith. They were very carefully checked and verified before being recorded. The verification process included an analysis of the chain of transmission to ensure that fake Hadiths that had crept in over the years, since the death of Muhammad[P], would be screened out. The most authentic, and the most widely used, collections are the ones compiled by the scholars Bukhari and Muslim. Other well known collections were compiled by An-Nasa'i, Abu Dawood, Tirmizi, and ibn-Majah.

## Examples of Hadith

Many Hadith volumes have been compiled that contain extensive information about how Muhammad[P] lived his life and what he said. The following are some examples of Muhammad[P]'s sayings:

- ❑ God has no mercy on one who has no mercy for others
- ❑ He who eats his fill while his neighbor goes without food is not a believer
- ❑ God does not judge according to your bodies and appearances but He scans your hearts and looks into your deeds
- ❑ There is a reward for kindness to every living thing
- ❑ It is obligatory upon a Muslim that he should listen to the ruler appointed over him and obey him whether he likes it or not, except when he is ordered to do a sinful thing. If he is ordered to do a sinful act, a Muslim should neither listen to him nor should he obey his orders.
- ❑ The one who looks after and works for a widow and for a poor person is like a warrior fighting for Allah's cause
- ❑ Allah will not be merciful to those who are not merciful to mankind

# ISLAMIC LAW: SHARIA

## Sources of Islamic religious authority

The basic principle of Islamic Law, also known as the Sharia, is that everything must be governed according to God's commands. There are two primary sources that comprise the Sharia: Koran and Sunnah. The Sharia, in a Muslim society, extends beyond interpreting simple religious issues and encompasses all aspects of life—individual and collective.

## Additional Shia authority

In addition to the Koran and Sunnah, which are recognized by all Muslims, Shias recognize a third source of authority which is based upon the teachings of 12 imams. The imams are the descendants of Ali ibn Abu Talib—Muhammad[P]'s son-in-law and the fourth caliph. Shias believe that the teachings and examples of the 12 imams are as authoritative as the Koran and the Sunnah. At the lower level, religious authority is vested in the ayatollahs.

## Role of the companions

The companions of Muhammad[P] were principled men of high character who faced deep hostility when they converted to Islam. Muslims look to them as role models and, where possible, try to emulate their behavior in situations where a Sunnah is not available. For example, knowledgeable Muslims consider Umar, the second caliph, to be the role model who set an example of how the religious sites of other religions should be treated. After the Muslims conquered Jerusalem, he went to visit a Christian church there. While Umar was at the church he refused to pray there, even though it was time for ritual prayers, because he did not want to create a precedent of praying there. Umar feared that, in the future, intolerant Muslims could use his precedent as a pretext to pray at the church and effectively take it over.

## Sharia Law

In Islam, there is no separation of Church and State and, hence, Islamic Law or the Sharia extends to every sphere including government, legislature, civil, public, and personal. The Sharia, which interprets issues using Islamic principles, covers every aspect of life in a Muslim society—individual and collective.

The primary source used for the Sharia Law's guiding principles is the Koran. The basic interpretation principle is that nothing in the Koran can be overruled or bypassed. A Muslim society has the freedom to legislate any new law provided it is not in conflict with the Koran or the Sunnah. However, no one has the authority to allow anything that God has specifically prohibited or, conversely, prohibit anything that God has allowed. All Koranic laws are binding and not subject to any interpretation, unless there is some ambiguity.

## Application of Sharia Law

The Sharia controls and regulates almost every facet of a Muslim's life. The subjects that it covers include, but are not limited, to the following:

- ❏ Basis for relations between God and man
- ❏ Relations between Muslims and non-Muslims
- ❏ Organization of a Muslim society
- ❏ Government
- ❏ Ethics
- ❏ Public and private behavior
- ❏ Individual behavior
- ❏ Relations and interaction with others
- ❏ Personal hygiene
- ❏ Civil and criminal issues
- ❏ Diet
- ❏ Rights of women
- ❏ Sexual conduct
- ❏ Rules for worship
- ❏ Resolution of conflicts

In addition to guiding an individual's personal behavior, Sharia Law can be applied in a broader context. It can be used to guide an individual's behavior with society as well as interactions between groups. The Sharia Law can also be used to settle disputes between nations, or within nations, as well as conflicts and wars. The Sharia Law does not exclude knowledge from other sources and is viewed by Muslims as a vehicle to solve diverse problems including personal, civil, criminal, and international.

## Crime and punishment in Islam

According to Islam, while all crimes will be punished in the hereafter, some crimes also need to be punished in this world. According to Islamic Law, crimes can be categorized under three main groups:

❑ Most serious which are called Had. They are against God's laws and include murder, apostasy, adultery, and theft.

❑ Least serious which are called Tazir. They are crimes against society and are equivalent to minor felonies or misdemeanors.

❑ Revenge crimes restitution which are called Qesas.

If a specific crime has a specific punishment prescribed in the Koran, a lesser or greater sentence cannot be imposed according to Islamic Law. Many of the Had crimes have fixed punishments. In general, punishments for Had crimes are severe. For example, theft can be punished by amputating the hand, depending on how many times the crime was committed, or by imprisonment. However, Islam requires a very high level of proof, especially for the most serious crimes. For example, four witnesses are required to prove adultery.

In Islamic Law, except for Had crimes, a judge is not bound by precedents or earlier decisions. Often, the punishments are a reflection of local customs and how conservative, or liberal, the society is. The same crime, such as bribery or drinking alcohol, may be punished differently in Saudi Arabia, Egypt, and Indonesia—all Muslim countries.

The punishment for Qesas crimes, which is based upon retribution and retaliation, is specified in the Koran. If a Qesas crime has been committed, such as pre-meditated murder, then the victim's family has the right to seek either Qesas punishment or Diya—which is financial restitution. If murder was committed due to a mistake, then only Diya is allowed—not Qesas.

## Interpretation of Sharia: Fiqh or Islamic jurisprudence

As Muslims faced new challenges after the death of Muhammad[P], the need developed to find solutions and answers to new problems and issues. It led to the development of a system of jurisprudence—the third source of law. Its objective was to simultaneously:

❑ Safeguard the foundations of Islamic Law embodied in the Koran and the Sunnah
❑ Provide flexibility so that potential new legal issues for Muslims could be addressed

Such needs led to the development of "Fiqh", meaning understanding or comprehension, that refers to the jurisprudence developed to interpret and implement the Sharia. It is based on four tools of jurisprudence:

❑ Koran
❑ Hadith
❑ Consensus (Ijma)
❑ Analogy (Qiyas)

To arrive at a solution for a problem, the first source to be tapped is the Koran. If an answer is not found there, the next source to be tapped is the Hadith. If there is no clear answer from the first two tools, consensus is used, which is based upon finding an agreement from other sources—such as Muhammad[P]'s companions and others who immediately followed them. If even Ijma provides no answer, then an analogy or something comparable is used as the basis for arriving at a decision..

There are four schools of Islamic jurisprudence which are named after their founders: Hanafi, Shafi'i, Maliki, and Hanbali. Even though they use the same sources for making their judgments, the four schools have come up with different interpretations regarding various issues. However, it should be noted that on major and fundamental issues, there is agreement between all four schools. There also exists a fifth school, known as Jafari, that is followed by the Shia sect.

## Status of Sharia in Muslim countries

There exist many movements in Muslim countries whose objective is to discard their existing legal system and make Sharia the law of the country. However, they have not had much support and, in fact, have generated a lot of controversy. Opponents say that they cannot implement punishments, such as cutting off a hand, in an existing unjust society. Their argument is that such laws were implemented in a just and generous society where there was no reason to steal. Therefore, unless such societies elevate themselves to a level where the incentive for crimes is gone, and hungry people are not forced to steal food, it does not make sense to implement such punishments.

At this time, most Muslim countries implement a hybrid of Sharia and civil laws. Typically, in such countries, the implementation of Sharia is restricted to personal and family matters such as marriage, divorce, and inheritance.

# ISLAMIC GOVERNMENT
## Objective of an Islamic state

An Islamic State has the following objectives:
- ❑ Establish, maintain, and develop virtues that God desires in man
- ❑ Prevent and eradicate evils that God dislikes

In view of these two basic principles, it becomes obvious that the primary duty of an Islamic state is to implement and uphold God's laws as stated in the Koran and clarified in the Sunnah. Such a state must be driven by the need to do everything as per God's commandments and the requirements of justice, rather than any expediency.

## Basis of Islamic political system

An Islamic state's political system is based on three principles:
- ❑ Tawheed—oneness of God
- ❑ Prophethood
- ❑ Caliphate

The principle of Tawheed dictates that only God can be the ruler and, consequently, His commands are the law which must be followed by society. In an Islamic state, it means that all its laws must be based upon, or conform to, God's commandments.

The principle of prophethood dictates that an Islamic state should follow the Sunnah because Muhammad[P] provided an example and the model for implementing Islamic laws in everyday life. In combination with the primary source, the Koran, it means that the state must follow the Sharia.

The caliphate is just an instrument, chosen by the people, for the implementation of God's laws within prescribed limits. A ruler cannot exercise any authority that is in conflict with the Sharia.

## Meaning of democracy In Islam

In an Islamic society, a government or ruling body can only be formed with the approval of its constituents—all of whom have the same rights. The head of the government can continue in office only till he retains the confidence of the people. Every citizen has the right to criticize the leader and/or his government. All citizens should have reasonable means available to them for the ventilation of their opinions.

## Leadership

The administration of an Islamic state's government is the responsibility of its leader, who is called the caliph (khalifa) or amir. Such a position is not hereditary. An amir, who has to be elected by the people, is expected to have both religious and political responsibilities. He is accountable to his people and can retain power only so long as he enjoys their confidence. An amir is advised and assisted by the Shoora, an advisory council elected by the people. It is incumbent upon an amir to govern his country in accordance with the Shoora's advice.

## Legislation

In an Islamic society, new laws can be legislated by legislative bodies so long as they do not conflict with the Sharia. The members of such bodies must be elected and represent the people, whose confidence they must retain in order to remain in office.

# CHAPTER 7
# ISLAMIC MORALS SYSTEM AND MUSLIM CHARACTERISTICS

## WHAT THE ISLAMIC SYSTEM IS BASED UPON

### Morals system

According to Islam, the objective of man's life is to worship God and to please Him. Such an objective can only be achieved by a high standard of morality, whose importance was underlined by Muhammad[P] who said, "Best among you is who is best in his character."

Islam attempts to inculcate in man the love as well as fear of God. The expectation is that once a person is fully aware of God and what He desires, and can differentiate between good and bad, he will make a conscientious effort to achieve a high level of morality—which is pleasing to God.

The Islamic morals system is primarily based upon God's commandments and laws as described in the Koran. In conjunction with the Islamic legal system, it protects the broad ranging fundamental rights that it guarantees all human beings. Since the morals system is based upon the Koran, it is permanent and not subject to change based upon the perceived needs of the day. It is immune to any changes that a government or society may want to introduce. However, while its core principles cannot be tampered with, Islam is flexible enough to adapt and accommodate reasonable changes, when required.

## What the Islamic system encompasses

The Islamic system is based upon traditional moral values that are universally accepted. However, it differs from other systems in that it covers all aspects of a man's life—from cradle to grave. It covers the personal, religious, social, legal, economic, political, individual, and collective aspects of his life. In the Islamic system, superiority is not based upon a person's wealth, power, nationality, status in society, physical attributes, etc. Instead, it is based upon righteousness—piety and good conduct.

## How system is to be implemented

Islam aims to provide a practical and realistic moral system that can be implemented in the daily life of a human being throughout his life. It aims to promote virtues such as honesty, responsibility, fairness, justice, mercy, generosity, kindness, hard work, integrity, patience, steadfastness, modesty, control of passions, charity, etc. It seeks to get rid of dishonesty, tyranny, injustice, irresponsibility, hatred, treachery, backbiting, selfishness as well as other vices. It seeks the promotion of a system that encourages good behavior and penalizes wrong deeds.

The Islamic moral standards and ethical codes are required to be implemented with sincerity and at all times. They cannot be altered, or suspended, to suit any personal or temporary expediency.

# PERSONALITY AND BEHAVIORAL CHARACTERISTICS

## Spiritual

The objective of any act of worship in Islam, ritual or non-ritual, is to become conscious of God. A Muslim needs to have a mindset that always makes him aware that he is in the presence of God. Islam views God-consciousness as the state that will lead God to reward, in this world as well as in the hereafter, the person who exhibits that characteristic.

Since Islam covers all aspects of a person's life, God-consciousness is not limited to the ritual acts of worship. Instead, it extends to all spheres of life. Therefore, any act which is performed with the objective of pleasing God, if it does not conflict with His commandments, is considered to be an act of worship. The act can be as simple as holding the door open for someone or simply saying thank you, provided it is performed with the intention of pleasing God who likes man to perform good and virtuous acts. Islam encourages its followers to remember God, and thank Him, at every opportunity such as:
- ❑ Before starting to eat and after finishing eating
- ❑ When meeting someone
- ❑ When noticing a phenomenon such as sunrise or sunset
- ❑ When entering a mosque
- ❑ When about to drive

Islam seeks to strive for balance in man's life. It wants man to be fearful of God and also believe in His mercy. Such an attitude is based on the logic that if there is no fear, then evil will not be prevented and there will be too much sin. Fear is created by making man realize the horrible punishment of hell. On the other hand, if there is no forgiveness, then a sinner will despair if he realizes his mistakes. Therefore, God lays out the hope of forgiveness as stated in the Koran, "Despair not of the mercy of Allah: Verily, Allah forgives all sins. Truly, He is Oft-Forgiving, Most Merciful (39:53)."

## Personal

The following sections describe some of the personal qualities that Muslims are expected to have or, when they are lacking, strive for.

## Self-respect

A Muslim does not believe that he has to be subservient to anyone except God. Such belief ensures in him a strong sense of self-respect and lack of fear of human beings. His honor and dignity are shaped by his view of where he stands in God's eyes, rather than what a fellow human thinks of him. Consequently, he will not do anything in life that will lower his own self-respect or cause him to fall from God's grace.

## Purity and chastity

Muslims men and women are required to be chaste, modest, and self-respecting. Such characteristics apply to their behavior, dress, speech as well as appearance. Muslims are expected to abhor anything impure or degrading and to:

❑ Stay away from drunkenness, adultery, homosexuality, and lack of chastity
❑ Keep away from lewdness—both in public and in private
❑ Avoid displaying their bodies
❑ Avoid overt sexual behavior
❑ Stress the dignity and honor of women
❑ Avoid free and casual social mixing of the sexes
❑ Show reserve and modesty in the company of the opposite sex
❑ Practice chastity before and after marriage

## Cleanliness

There is significant emphasis on cleanliness in Islam—physical and spiritual. According to the Koran, "Allah loves those who turn to Him constantly and He loves those who keep themselves pure and clean (2:222)." On the physical side, Muslims are required to keep in a clean condition their body, clothes, home, and community. According to the Hadith, "Cleanliness is half of the faith." A constant state of purity is encouraged. A ritual prayer cannot be performed unless the body is clean. To prepare for each of the five daily ritual prayers, a Muslim is required to wash his face, hands, arms, and feet.

# Social

## *What social responsibility encompasses*

There are two aspects of the teachings of Islam that cover this area. They are the:
❑ Rights of God: this includes God's claims on man as well as his duties and obligations to God
❑ Rights of men: this includes rights on each other as well as corresponding obligations and social responsibilities

Islam teaches social responsibility that is based on kindness and consideration for others. Such responsibility covers a wide circle and encompasses:
❑ Family members
❑ Relatives
❑ Neighbors
❑ Friends and acquaintances
❑ Needy people such as orphans and widows
❑ Community
❑ Environment, animals, etc.

If a person infringes on the rights of someone else, and no amends are made in this life, then the wrong-doer will have to repay the wronged person on the Day of Judgment. On that day, good deeds from the wrong-doer will be given to the wronged person or the bad deeds from the wronged person will be transferred to the wrong-doer.

## *Charity*

Islam stresses the giving of charity to those in society who are needy and disadvantaged. It expects Muslims to pay zakat, which is mandatory for those who meet the eligibility requirements, as well as sadaqa which is optional. It encourages helping the less fortunate as much as possible. Charity, as viewed by Islam, means more than just making a donation in cash or in kind. It considers acts that do good for others, such as removing a road hazard, as being equivalent to charity.

## *Brotherliness*

Islam inculcates a feeling of brotherhood among Muslims by making them consider themselves as part of a united Muslim brotherhood or Ummah. A Muslim is expected to wish and desire the same for other Muslims as he would for himself. He is expected to share their joy as well as grief.

## *Helping nature*

A Muslim is expected to be helpful to all human beings around him without any consideration for their religion, culture, ethnicity, social standing or other factors.

## *Relationship between old and young*

Islam enjoins its followers to be affectionate to those who are younger. On the other hand, those who are younger are expected to be respectful to those who are older. According to the Hadith, "Whoever does not be merciful to his younger or whoever does not respect his elder, he is not among us."

# Family

## *Importance of family*

The family is the most important social unit of every society. A weak family system is the root cause of many ills that are plaguing modern society. Islam clearly recognized that, centuries ago, and defined the rights of family members with the aim of making it society's foundation. It promotes behavior that is based on love, mutual respect, unselfish behavior, consideration, and generosity. A Muslim is expected to recognize and respect the importance and role of the family in creating and maintaining an Islamic environment.

## *Relationship between parents and children*

Islam views the relationship between parents and children as being very important. Therefore, it has clearly specified the responsibilities and duties of both parents and children. Parents are required to provide an upbringing that gives their children a solid foundation in the Islamic way of life. They have to teach them Islamic characteristics, values, morals, behavior, and attitude.

Islam also emphasizes that children should respect and obey their parents. Muslims are enjoined to be kind to their parents and to honor them. Islam teaches that children should take care of their parents when they are old. Taking care of elderly parents is considered morally and spiritually uplifting by Muslims.

## *Relationship with other relatives*

Islam enjoins Muslims to discharge the due rights of their relatives. They are expected to take care of, or help, needy and old relatives and be kind to them. They are also expected to treat their grandparents just like their own parents.

# Intellectual

## Knowledge

Knowledge is the quality that placed man above the angels and, therefore, its enhancement is encouraged by Islam. The first verse of the Koran revealed to Muhammad[P] was, "Read in the name of your Lord Who created (96-1)", which implies reading, learning, researching, and observing. Islam urges its followers to read, write, and seek knowledge from wherever they can get it. A Muslim is expected to seek religious knowledge, which will guide him in performing deeds that will help on the Day of Judgment, as well as secular knowledge.

Throughout the Koran, man is encouraged to observe and appreciate God's creations—sun, moon, night, day, etc. He is encourage to use his reasoning and research to arrive at conclusions. In the Koran, God enjoins Muslims to pray to Him for knowledge, "O my Lord ! increase me in knowledge (20:114)." The following Hadith also stress knowledge:

❑ Acquisition of knowledge is obligatory on every Muslim man and woman
❑ Seek knowledge even if it means going to China
❑ Knowledge or wisdom is the lost wealth of the believers (so whenever you find it, take it)

## No limits are specified

Contrary to some misconceptions, Islam encourages education in science and technology. Muslims of the Golden Age excelled in many fields including medicine, chemistry, physics, astronomy, and mathematics. The

Muslims' decline in education and, especially in various scientific fields, can be traced to the decline of the Islamic Empires in the last millennium.

There is no limit to the knowledge that a Muslim can gain so long as it conforms to the doctrine of God's oneness. Certain controversial fields such as abortion and human cloning, which are against the basic principles of Islam, are considered taboo areas for Muslims.

# Economic

## Work

Muslims are expected to earn their living through honest and hard work. Any type of physical or intellectual work is permissible, and honorable, so long as it is lawful and in harmony with Islamic goals and values. Any work connected with prohibited activities such as gambling, prostitution, producing or distributing alcohol are considered illegal. A Muslim is not permitted to avoid working, due to devoting his life to worship, and live off charity. Islam recognizes the:
- ❑ Right to work
- ❑ Right to the product of that work

## Property

Islam recognizes the following rights:
- ❑ Right to private property
- ❑ Right of inheritance

Muslims are allowed to engage in business and trading. Islam permits the ownership of private property so long as it is acquired by honest and legal means. Private property can be used in any way so long as it is lawful and not detrimental to the community or society. It is expected that a Muslim will not use personal property exclusively for personal use and benefit. Where possible, it is recommended that personal property be used for providing benefit to the needy and the community.

## Wealth

Islam permits the acquiring of wealth. However, pride in one's wealth, miserliness, and greed are considered sins. According to the Islamic perspective, the more wealth that a person has, greater is his responsibility to use it in the best possible way. A Muslim is viewed as only a temporary custodian of any wealth that he accumulates, which actually belongs to God as per Islamic belief. Islam reminds man that he has to return to God, ultimately, with nothing except his deeds. Therefore, what is important is how he earned his wealth, rather than the amount that he earned. According to Islam, this principle, if followed, will ensure the development of a just society.

## Business principles

Islam mandates that businesses be run on the same moral principles as individual lives. In other words, they must be based on high moral principles. Islam prohibits dishonesty, fraud, deceit or misrepresentation in business. It encourages the concept of free enterprise and socially responsible capitalism. However, it also stresses social responsibility and concern for employees.

Islam prohibits the selling of goods and services that are illegal, called haram in Arabic. It prohibits gambling, lotteries, and businesses associated with the sale and distribution of alcohol. Also considered illegal are any activities that promote, and encourage, people to do something that is considered haram. Among prohibited activities are:

❏ Hoarding and price gouging by artificially reducing supply, especially food
❏ Price manipulation

❑ Interference in the free market
❑ Government price control except in exceptional circumstances
❑ Buying stolen property
❑ Raising pigs or cultivating plants such as poppy and hashish

Islam permits profits so long as they are halal (legal) and not haram (illegal). Interest is a form of profit and most Islamic scholars consider it to be prohibited. However, some scholars differentiate between interest and usury. According to them, only usury is prohibited.

A Muslim is required to honor his obligations and pay his debts. He is expected to keep his word, and act in accordance with Islamic principles and morals, when dealing with business and economic issues. He cannot separate ethics and religion from his day-to-day life either in the personal or business sphere. Despite such high moral expectations from Muslims, Islam recommends that, wherever possible, agreements and contracts should documented be in writing.

# ADDITIONAL CHARACTERISTICS

## Sincerity

A Muslim is required to be sincere to God as well as other human beings. Unless a person is sincere towards God, his relationship with Him cannot exist. There is no purpose in pretending to be worshipping God, and going through the motions of worship, unless one is honest and sincere. Sincerity is also required in one's relationship with other human beings. Islam enjoins one to be free of hypocrisy, envy, selfishness and other traits that prevent a person from being straightforward with others.

## Equality

Islam considers all humans as being equal. In the eyes of God, everyone is equal whether they are men, women, black, white, royalty, ordinary citizens, Arabs or non-Arabs. The only criteria for differentiation is their righteousness. Each and every human being has direct and equal access to God. Therefore, based on the simple principle that God treats everyone equally, it becomes incumbent upon Muslims to act in the same way towards other human beings.

## Individual responsibility

A true Muslim accepts God and his commandments. With that acceptance comes individual responsibility for each and every action that he takes throughout his life. If a person does not accept individual responsibility, in any sphere of life, he cannot expect to be successful. Islam expects every Muslim to act responsibly because he, and no one else, will be held accountable for his actions in this world. This characteristic, of individual responsibility, is one of the most important that a Muslim is required to have.

## Honesty

Muslims are expected to have very high moral standards and be very honest in all their dealings. A Muslim will not:
- Offer or take a bribe
- Cheat or steal
- Break an oath, pledge or a promise
- Break a trust
- Take a false oath
- Give false evidence

## Truthfulness

Muhammad[P] taught his followers to always be truthful and to avoid hypocrisy. According to him, the big jehad is to speak the truth before the tyrant king. He taught Muslims to speak out if they see freedom, truth, and justice being compromised. He preached that if they see something wrong they must, depending on what they can do as a minimum, act in one of the following ways:

- ❏ Rectify the situation through some action, deed or conduct
- ❏ Oppose verbally
- ❏ Disapprove silently through an expression
- ❏ Disapprove in the heart

In the view of Islam, there are two categories of hypocrisy:

- ❏ Hypocrisy in belief
- ❏ Hypocrisy in deeds and actions

The following are some attributes of a hypocrite that Islam considers sinful:

- ❏ Lying
- ❏ Breaking promises
- ❏ Betraying
- ❏ Treachery
- ❏ False excuses
- ❏ Outward behavior that contradicts what is in the heart
- ❏ Causing mischief while claiming to establish peace
- ❏ Finding fault with God's decree
- ❏ Saying prayers hastily or being lazy in worship
- ❏ Concern for the outward appearance and neglect of the inner condition

## Justice

A Muslim is expected to resist injustice with all available means. By the same token, a Muslim must never be unjust. When retaliating, which is considered justifiable, one cannot exceed limits. In other words, the retaliation must not exceed the injustice that was originally perpetrated.

## Courtesy

A Muslim is expected to treat others as he would like to be treated himself. Therefore, he must be courteous and polite to others. Whenever he meets someone, he should greet that person. If he is returning a greeting, he must be equally courteous—if not more.

## Forgiveness

Muslims are taught that God is very forgiving and merciful because He realizes that human beings make mistakes all the time. Therefore, if they repent sincerely, they can expect God to forgive any sin with the exception of the gravest sin—shirk. Hence, Muslims are also encouraged to be forgiving of the wrongs that others commit against them.

## Speech

A Muslim is expected to control his tongue and always be careful about what he says. He is not allowed to use foul language and profanity, be bad tempered, or engage in gossip and slander. A Muslim is expected to be polite when speaking, even when aggravated and angry.

## Preaching

Muslims are not expected to limit the practice of Islam to their personal lives. They are expected to spread the word of Islam through preaching, which can be accomplished in many ways. It can include explaining Islam to friends and acquaintances, inviting non-Muslims to special religious events, accompanying missionary groups, etc. Muslims are encouraged to become models that non-Muslims can observe and be impressed with.

## Avoiding waste

A good Muslim will not waste his wealth by extravagant spending because Islam recommends moderation. It also encourages giving to charity. However, if a donor donates too much, which leaves nothing for the necessities of life, it is considered equivalent to the wasting of wealth. A Muslim is expected to strike a balance between too much spending (squandering) and too little spending (greed and miserliness).

## Other virtues

There are a number of additional good characteristics and deeds that are expected of Muslims. They include patience, contentment, humility, gratefulness, generosity, mercy, and hospitality. The characteristics that Muslims must avoid include lying, backbiting, slandering, flattery, dishonesty, cheating, deceiving, selfishness, hard heartedness, miserliness, and revenge. They are also expected to avoid being vain, bad tempered, foul mouthed, malicious, and disrespectful.

# CHAPTER 8
# BAD DEEDS, DAY-TO-DAY LIVING, AND COMMON ISSUES

## RECOGNIZING RIGHT AND WRONG

### How actions are judged

The fundamental principles governing morals and behavior in Islam are:

❑ Actions are judged by reference, in sequence, to the Koran, Sunnah, and Muhammad[P]'s companions. If no precedent is found in these three sources, then one is free to judge using the logic of benefit (or harm) and by determining whether it is natural (or unnatural)

❑ Anything beneficial to man's spiritual well-being is permitted

❑ Anything harmful to man is prohibited including acts that:

  o lower a man's dignity, degrades him or damages his body or soul

  o harm the society

In Islam, actions are judged based on the following categories:

❑ Mandatory

❑ Recommended

❑ Neutral

❑ Disapproved

❑ Forbidden

Violation of the mandatory requirements, such as the five daily obligatory prayers and fasting during Ramadan, are considered to be serious sins. In such cases, according to Islam, violators will be punished by God. They can also be punished by the Islamic state. However, at this time, implementation of Islamic laws and punishments varies from country to country. Typically, local laws and the strictness in implementing Islamic Law, with its associated punishments, reflect local attitudes and the area's conservative or liberal leanings.

Failure to perform recommended or neutral acts is not penalized. Forbidden acts such as murder, adultery, and drinking alcohol are required to be punished according to Islamic Law. However, if they are not punished, then a violation of Islamic principles takes place by those in authority who choose to ignore such violations.

## Recognizing polytheism

Acts that are forbidden according to Islam are specified in the Koran. Additional forbidden acts are listed in the Sunnah. The degree of sin associated with those acts varies considerably, with polytheism being considered the worst. The worship of any creation and ascribing partners to God is unforgivable in Islam. Polytheism can take various forms and include:

- ❑ Shirk by association: includes association with gods, spirits, saints, humans, etc.
- ❑ Shirk by negation: refers to the denial of God—as in atheism
- ❑ Shirk by humanization: refers to giving God the attributes of human beings and animals, as is done by Hindus and Buddhists; also refers to those who view Jesus as God incarnate
- ❑ Shirk by deification: refers to assigning God's names or attributes to His creations
- ❑ Major shirk: involves praying to someone other than God; this is the worst type of sin which is unforgivable

❑ Minor shirk: involves performing an act of worship, such as giving charity or performing a prayer, to show off or gain fame rather than to please God

❑ Inconspicuous shirk: indicates dissatisfaction with God's ordained conditions

# SINS AND REPENTANCE

A Muslim is required to keep himself free from every kind of evil, wickedness, and sin. He is also expected to share his knowledge with others. Therefore, Muslims are encouraged to preach to others, Muslims and non-Muslims, that they should abstain from all activities that are considered sinful by Islam.

## Sins among the worst

Various Islamic scholars have compiled a list of the 70 sins that Islam considers the worst. The following is a partial list of sins extracted from that master list:

❑ Associating partners with God
❑ Forging statements concerning God or His messenger
❑ Denying God's decree
❑ Believing in fortune-tellers and astrologers
❑ Murder
❑ Suicide
❑ Fornication and adultery
❑ Homosexuality
❑ Usury
❑ Drinking alcohol
❑ Gambling
❑ Stealing and robbery
❑ Being a habitual liar
❑ Eating carrion, blood or pork
❑ Devouring the wealth of orphans
❑ Not praying
❑ Not paying zakat
❑ Not fasting during Ramadan without a valid reason

- Not performing Hajj, while being able to do so
- Continuously missing Friday prayers without a valid excuse
- Disobeying parents
- Cutting off ties with relatives
- Harming neighbors or Muslims
- Practicing witchcraft and magic
- Giving false testimony
- Consuming wealth acquired unlawfully
- Bribery
- Betrayal of trust and backstabbing
- Not fulfilling one's promises
- Being arrogant, boastful, and vain
- Cursing others
- Arguing or quarreling for show and not seeking the truth

- Being deceitful or deceptive
- Eavesdropping
- Backbiting and spreading harmful stories
- Slandering chaste women
- Woman being rebellious to her husband
- Wrongdoing, deception or oppression by a ruler
- Committing injustice
- Committing oppression
- Overbearing or taking advantage of the wife and those who are weak
- Levying illegal taxes
- Acquiring knowledge only for worldly gain
- Concealing knowledge
- Reminding people of one's kindness

## Additional sins

The following list includes sins that have been prohibited in the Koran and are described as the "deeds of the people of hell":
- Disbelieving in His messengers
- Inconsistency between what is in one's heart and what one shows to people (hypocrisy)

❑  Despairing of the mercy of Allah
❑  Fearing a creation instead of the Creator
❑  Going against the Koran and Sunnah in word or deed
❑  Obeying a creation in an act of disobedience to the Creator
❑  To do or aid any kind of dishonest, unethical or immoral act
❑  Malicious envy
❑  Treachery
❑  Miserliness

## Repentance and atonement

Muslims view God as very merciful because He has promised to forgive if a sinner turns to Him for repentance. According to Islam, a person's sins are forgiven provided the following conditions are met:

❑  Sins are acknowledged
❑  There is sincere regret for the committed sins
❑  There is sincere resolve that the sins will not be repeated
❑  If a sin harmed someone, an attempt will be made to rectify the harm that was done

# DAY-TO-DAY LIVING

## Drinking and eating regulations

The basic principle in Islam is that any food can be eaten unless it has been specifically prohibited. The prohibited items are few and they include the following:

❑  Alcohol and its by-products
❑  Pork and its by-products
❑  Narcotic and additive drugs
❑  Meat of dead and carnivorous animals

❑ Blood
❑ Birds of prey such as eagles and vultures
❑ Any animal that is slaughtered without invoking God's name; Muslims can only eat halal (kosher) meat, which is the meat of an animal that has been slaughtered while invoking God's name

Islam teaches that one should be thankful to God for providing food. Wasting food is considered a sin. As part of the Islamic tradition, Muslims remember God before and after eating anything. Before eating, a Muslim says "Bismillah (in the name of Allah)". A typical supplication after a meal is, "All praise is for Allah who gave us this food and drink and who made us Muslims."

## Modesty and dress code

The Islamic dress code emphasizes modesty. Men are mandated to cover their body from the knee to the navel. For women, the requirement is to wear clothes that are not too tight or transparent. They are required to cover all parts of their body except the hands and face.

The primary objective of the dress code is to prevent women from becoming the object of enticement or desire. The dress code inside the home, or in the company of relatives, is more liberal and women can dress more casually and also keep their heads uncovered. A woman can also wear jewelry as well as expensive and fancy clothes. However, they are only to be used for displaying to the husband or relatives—not other men.

In many Muslim countries, women cover their faces with some sort of a veil. The style of this covering varies from country to country. In Afghanistan, the burqa is of the shroud type, while two different veil styles are used in the Indian subcontinent and the United Arab Emirates. There is disagreement among Islamic scholars in the interpretation of some

Koranic verses, particularly 33:59 and 24:31, regarding the subject of covering the face. The liberal interpretation is that they do not require the face to be covered.

## Relations between men and women

Islam prohibits any sex except between married couples. With the objective of preventing pre-marital and extra-marital sex, and limiting the opportunities for temptation, it tries to limit the intimate mixing of males and females. As part of its effort, Islam provides specific as well as general rules and guidelines. For example, it prohibits free and casual social gatherings between men and women. It also restricts private meetings, that allow them to be alone, between a man and a woman unless they are married or related.

There is, however, no restriction on women working in an environment that includes males. It may be pertinent to point out that before he became a prophet, Muhammad[P] was employed by a woman who, later on, became his wife. After Muhammad[P] was initiated into prophethood, no restrictions were imposed on women being able to work.

## Halal and haram

The halal (legal) and haram (illegal) restrictions are based upon specific God's commandments which cannot be legislated upon by any human being. In Islam, some clear guidelines have been issued regarding what is halal and what is haram. The basic principle is that if something has not been prohibited, it is permissible. It should be pointed out that very few items have been prohibited. A secondary principle is that if something is illegal or haram, anything that might lead to it is also considered haram and prohibited. For example, while drinking alcohol is prohibited, Islam also prohibits all activities that are associated with the production, storage, and transportation of alcohol.

Another principle is that the intention of the doer, which may be very noble, cannot override the illegality of a prohibited action and, hence, such an action remains illegal. For example, giving charity using illegally gained wealth does not negate the sins accumulated due to the illegal accumulation of that wealth. This is in contrast with the good intentions of a person that converts a permissible action into an act of worship.

According to the doctrine of necessity, a prohibited item can be used if there is dire necessity—such as the need to save one from death. For example, a man dying of hunger in the desert can eat a pig if his life depended upon it. In the case of a medicine that contains alcohol, it may be taken provided there is no available medicine that can be used as a substitute.

## Doing more than the basic requirements

A good Muslim is expected to go beyond the basic Islamic requirements and do whatever he can to please God. The following are some of the ways in which additional acts can be undertaken by Muslims for earning more rewards:

- ❑ Performing more than the mandatory five daily prayers
- ❑ Giving charity in excess of the mandatory zakat
- ❑ Fasting additional days over the course of the year
- ❑ Performing as many good deeds as possible
- ❑ Performing social work
- ❑ Performing Daawah—inviting others to Islam

# MODERN DAY ISSUES

## Abortion

According to Islam, the killing of born as well as unborn children is prohibited. It does not permit the destruction of any life or an embryo at any stage of its development. Therefore, Islam does not permit abortion, which it equates to murder. Islam considers abortion to be an act that is worse than burying alive, which the pagan Arabs used to do. An exception is permitted in the case where a mother's life is in danger due to continuation of the pregnancy. Also prohibited are abortion pills like the RU-486.

## Artificial insemination

The artificial insemination procedure is considered acceptable in Islam only if the sperm donor is the recipient's husband. However, if the donor is anyone else, it is strictly prohibited. Artificial insemination is permitted while a valid marriage contract exists between the donor and the recipient. It is prohibited if a divorce has taken place or the donor is deceased. Artificial insemination by anyone, other than the husband, is considered to be a major sin equivalent to adultery.

## Surrogate motherhood

Surrogate motherhood can be described as "renting the womb." In this procedure, a surrogate mother bears a child for the benefit of another woman who is unable to do so. Typically, though not always, it is done in return for financial and material benefits. Since such a pregnancy takes place outside a marriage contract, it is considered illegitimate, degrading, and unacceptable. Surrogate motherhood is viewed as being a serious sin since it takes place in a scenario developed outside marriage, which is equivalent to adultery.

## Suicide

Suicide is viewed as a very serious sin by Islam because it considers all life to be sacred. According to Islam, no one has the right to take any life and, therefore, suicide is viewed as a crime equivalent to murder. According to a Hadith, Muhammad[P] said, "He who throws himself down from a rock and commits suicide will be throwing himself into the fire of hell; he who drinks poison and kills himself will have the poison in his hand, drinking it forever in the fire of hell and he who kills himself with a weapon will have that weapon in his hand, stabbing himself forever in the fire of hell."

Muslims are taught to be resolute and be prepared for the hardships and tests that God sends their way from time to time. Instead of running away from their problems, at such times, they are encouraged to pray to God to provide them strength, and His help, in dealing with their issues.

## Euthanasia

Euthanasia is the practice of ending a life when it becomes unbearable due to some terminal illness such as cancer. In Islam, patience and endurance are qualities that are highly regarded and rewarded. Islam prohibits the practice of euthanasia as, according to it, no man has the right to take his own or anyone else's life. Euthanasia is considered equivalent to suicide, prohibited, and an unforgivable sin. The person ending his life, as well as those aiding and enabling euthanasia, are considered sinners.

## Organ donation

According to many Muslim scholars, donating an organ is permissible provided it is done with the intention of saving someone's life. Even though violating a human body, living or dead, is impermissible, organ donation is considered permissible due to two rules:

❏ Necessities overrule prohibition
❏ Choice of the lesser of two evils if both are unavoidable (saving life versus preserving the body)

The organ donation procedure should not pose any risk to the life of the donor. The donor must also be willing to donate his organ and be free from any pressure. The practice of selling organs, in order to meet some financial needs, is considered sinful and prohibited.

## Homosexuality

Islam prohibits any sex outside of marriage including adultery, fornication, and homosexuality. It is very clear and unambiguous in characterizing homosexuality as a devious and serious sin. Homosexuality is considered to be a perverted corrupt act and a moral disorder. It is viewed as being a moral disease, unhealthy, unnatural, and a serious sin. References against homosexuality, which will be severely punished by God, are to be found in the Koran as well as the Sunnah.

## Cloning

Cloning is a relatively new issue about which Muslim scholars have not yet issued definitive rulings. Two factors that will impact the way Islamic scholars will view it are the process used to achieve it and the objective for which it is being carried out. Some scholars currently view it, based on the few known facts, as being impermissible. It is expected that there will be revisions to any known opinions as more facts and intentions become known. The obvious fear is that genetic engineering can be misused and manipulated through cloning.

## Stem cell research

The Islamic view on stem cells conforms with the Christian Church view that stem cell research in itself is not wrong. However, creating and/or destroying human life in order to mine stem cells is wrong. An American panel of experts, convened by the Islamic Institute, has supported stem cell research on spare embryos from in-vitro fertilization. According to them, research on stem cells taken from adults should be encouraged and that no in-vitro may be performed for the purpose of supplying stem cells for research.

According to the panel, whenever in-vitro is needed to deal with the problem of infertility, the sperm and ovum must be taken from a lawfully wed couple. It also concluded that "as fertility clinics are forced to fertilize more than one ovum so as to increase the chances of success, unused (embryo) may be used for research instead of destroying them, provided that it is done in the first few days after fertilization and provided further that the unused embryos are donated without any financial return." The Institute also noted, when issuing its ruling, that its opinion is subject to further enhancements based on presently unknown scientific developments.

# CHAPTER 9
# RIGHTS AND OBLIGATIONS

## RIGHTS OF GOD AND THE PROPHET

### Importance of respecting rights

A casual study of the world today will reveal that there is conflict at every level between individuals, groups, societies, and nations. A closer look will reveal that the basis for the overwhelming majority of conflicts is the denial of various rights: political, social, individual, legal, economic, and religious. Therefore, it is logical to conclude that for peace and harmonious living, and for societies to prosper, there must be universal fairness and respect for the rights of others.

A basic principle that Islam teaches Muslims is to respect and honor the rights of others and to discharge their corresponding obligations. For those who respect the rights of others, God has promised a reward in the hereafter. Islam specifies various rights that every man is entitled to, depending on his position. Those rights, which cannot be abrogated by anyone, are identified in the following sections.

### God's rights

According to Islam, the most important rights are the rights of God who created everything and also provided everything that every creation has. The only demands that God makes on man are to:

- ❑ Believe in the oneness of God
- ❑ Worship Him and no one else
- ❑ Surrender to Him completely
- ❑ Obey His commandments
- ❑ Thank Him for His blessings and show gratitude

## Prophet's rights

Muslims consider Muhammad[P] to be a great blessing whom God sent to guide man onto the right path that leads to heaven. They are expected to honor the following rights of Prophet Muhammad[P]:

- ❑ Obey his instructions and commands
- ❑ Emulate the way he led his life
- ❑ Love him and send their blessings

# OTHERS' RIGHTS AND OBLIGATIONS

## Children's rights and parents' obligations

The family is considered to be a very important element in the overall structure of society. For each of its members, Islam has defined specific rights and obligations. The obligations of parents, which correspond to the rights of children, include the following:

- ❑ Providing a religious upbringing
- ❑ Teaching high values
- ❑ Providing good education, especially Islamic
- ❑ Showing examples of Islamic behavior, manners, and morals
- ❑ Being kind to daughters
- ❑ Providing all children the same treatment
- ❑ Saying the call to prayer in the child's ear when it is born

❏ Celebrating aqeeqah when a child is born; it involves shaving off the hair on the new-born baby's head and sacrificing a goat; this is a recommended—not a mandatory practice
❏ Giving the child a good name
❏ Marrying them, if they can afford it financially

## Parents' rights and children's obligations

In Islam, the rights of children are balanced by their obligations to their parents. Their obligations include:
❏ Honor
❏ Respect
❏ Obedience
❏ Kindness
❏ Humility
❏ Service
❏ Care during old age
❏ Prayers for their parents' forgiveness and salvation after they die

According to Islam, God is pleased if one works towards the pleasure of one's parents. However, it is a major sin if parents are disobeyed, harmed, abused or insulted. In comparison to the father, the rights of the mother are considered to be greater. Even non-Muslim parents must be shown kindness, well treated, and obeyed unless they ask for something to be done that violates God's commands.

## Rights of other relatives

Islam also emphasizes the rights of other relatives, which include:
❏ Good treatment
❏ Love

❑ Sympathy
❑ Kindness and consideration

According to a Hadith, Muhammad[P] said that, "Whoever violates the rights of relatives, shall not go to Paradise." He enjoined Muslims to continue to fulfill their obligations in spite of how their relatives may be behaving towards them.

## Rights of husband and wife

Both the husband and wife have rights and corresponding duties that they are expected to discharge during their married life. They include the following:

❑ Husband's duties:
  o As head of the family, be responsible for all its financial needs
  o Protect the wife
  o Consider his wife a blessing
  o Provide love and esteem to wife
  o Show kindness to spouse
  o Provide for wife's comfort
  o Be patient when his wife makes a mistake
❑ Wife's duties:
  o Must regard her husband above all others
  o Be faithful
  o Be obedient and loyal
  o Be devoted
  o Try her best to please her husband

## Neighbors' rights

Muslim as well as non-Muslim neighbors have rights on Muslims according to the teachings of Islam. According to Muhammad[P]'s sayings, "He is

not a believer who eats his fill when his neighbor beside him is hungry."
Some of the neighbors' rights that have been specified include:
- ❏ Visiting them when they are sick
- ❏ Offering condolences and congratulations, depending on the occasion
- ❏ Not looking at their women with bad looks or desire
- ❏ Ignoring their mistakes
- ❏ Covering their faults
- ❏ Helping financially
- ❏ Providing guidance and imparting knowledge
- ❏ Not treating them badly
- ❏ Attending their funeral and participating in burial arrangements

## Rights of the disadvantaged

Islam has also specified the rights of those in society who are needy and disadvantaged. They include widows, orphans, weak, poor, destitute, and the downtrodden. Taking care of their needs is considered to be highly virtuous. Mistreating an orphan is viewed very negatively. Helping a widow or someone needy or distressed has been equated to doing jehad as per the Hadith. Muslims are also enjoined to visit needy people who are sick, arrange for their treatment, and feed those who are hungry.

## Rights of other Muslims

Islam very strongly emphasizes the concept of brotherhood among Muslims. It specifies the rights that Muslims have over each other as well as their mutual responsibilities. Due to the high standards that have been laid down, a Muslim cannot expect the following from another Muslim:
- ❏ Backbiting
- ❏ Hate
- ❏ Breaking of ties

❑ Lack of mercy and compassion
❑ Blood feuding

A Muslim can expect the following from a fellow Muslim:
❑ Personal aid
❑ Mutual love
❑ Help during distress
❑ Defense of honor and dignity
❑ Forgiveness of mistakes and failings as well as help in overcome shortcomings
❑ Prayers for the brother (just as one would for himself)
❑ Loyalty and sincerity
❑ Greetings when they meet
❑ Acceptance if an invitation is given
❑ Mutual advice
❑ Visit when he is sick
❑ Accompany his dead body to the cemetery

## Rights of others

Islam also specifies the rights of those who do not fall in the various categories listed in the previous sections. Such rights include the rights of all mankind and His creations including animals. They include rights, irrespective of which community one may belong to, such as sympathy, kindness, and compassion. According to a Hadith, "There is a reward for kindness to every living animal or human."

# ISLAMIC VIEW OF HUMAN RIGHTS

## Objective

Islam views all humans equally so far as the application of God's laws and justice are concerned. It does not favor a nation, tribe, country, race, ethnic group or gender. It emphases dignity and justice for all human beings. It recognizes the fact that if justice and human rights are denied in a society, it will live in conflict with God's commandments. Therefore, in such an environment, where basic fundamental rights guaranteed by God are abused or denied, Islam cannot flourish.

## Human rights are sanctioned by God

Islam specifies fundamental rights that must be respected, under all circumstances, in every country. Those rights have been granted by God and cannot be abrogated or changed by any human being. A person's country of residence, or its Islamic status, has no bearing on the human rights that must be honored based on God's laws which have universal applicability. The following are some fundamental rights that are recognized by Islam:

- Right to life and property
- Right to freedom
- Human blood cannot be shed without strong justification
- No one can be tortured or oppressed
- Protection of honor
- Honor is inviolable; insulting or making fun of others is not allowed
- No hungry or sick person can be denied food or treatment, even if he belongs to the enemy
- Right to equality; racism is not allowed
- Justice cannot be denied even to those who are hated

❑ Basic standard of life
❑ Not to insult or abuse other religions: "Revile not ye those whom they call upon besides Allah, lest they out of spite revile Allah in their ignorance (6:108)."

## Perception of Islamic intolerance: A disconnect

There is a common perception among non-Muslims, especially in the West, that Islam is an intolerant religion and that it does not respect human rights or the religious freedom of minorities. This perception is based on three reasons.

First, nowadays, many Muslim countries are run by dictators or royal families who do not respect freedom, democracy, or human rights. Their actions, even though they violate Islamic principles, are incorrectly associated with Islam which guarantees human rights and religious freedom to its minorities.

Second, the accusation that Islam was only spread by the sword and that most nations were forcibly converted. The facts do not support the accusation, especially in the most widely quoted examples. While it is true that Muslims made many conquests during their initial expansion, most of them were for restoring freedoms and getting rid of oppressors. During those expeditions, Muslims were driven by the zeal to spread the word of God. However, they did not force local populations to convert to Islam. Much later, some misguided rulers did force conversions in contravention of the injunction in the Koran, "There is no compulsion in religion" (2:256). The spread of Islam through such means was insignificant. However, it helped create the perception that Islam is intolerant even though it opposes any forced conversions.

Third, is the lack of knowledge among both Muslims and non-Muslims. For example, Genghis Khan is mistakenly believed to be a Muslim due to his last name—a common Muslim surname at this time. Both Genghis and his grandson Halagu, two of the most feared rulers in history, wrought death and destruction over vast areas that became part of the biggest empire in the world. Their names are associated with brutality, massacres, and intolerance. Halagu, first defeated Muslim countries or dynasties, committed atrocities wherever he went, but subsequently converted to Islam. Through association, Islam is perceived negatively due to acts committed by feared historical figures such as Halagu before their conversion to Islam.

# BASIC HUMAN RIGHTS SANCTIONED BY ISLAM

## Right to life

The right to live is man's first basic right. According to Islam, the life of every person is to be considered sacred. It prohibits the taking of any life except in the pursuit of justice. According to the Koran, the killing of an innocent person is equivalent to the killing of all mankind (and saving a life is considered equivalent to saving the life of all mankind). There is no exception for non-Muslims. According to Muhammad[P], "One who kills a man under covenant (non-Muslim citizen of an Islamic state), will not even smell the fragrance of paradise."

## Right to sanctity of property

Islam recognizes the right to private property and seeks to protect it. On the moral level, it makes stealing un-Islamic while also imposing deterrent punishments for the crime. Irrespective of whether a person is a Muslim or a non-Muslim, the life and property of all citizens in an Islamic state are considered sacred.

## Right to protection of honor

According to Islam, no person's honor should be abused. Therefore, it recognizes the right to protection from slander and ridicule. It seeks the avoidance of sarcasm, insults, name calling, backbiting, and defamation. Those who engage in spreading malicious stories or cast aspersions upon a woman's honor and chastity, which must be respected under all circumstances, are warned of punishment in both the worlds.

## Right to privacy and security

The sanctity and security of private life is recognized in Islam, which specifies rules to protect life in the home from interference. The Koran has specified that one should not enter any house unless the occupant's consent has been obtained. It also mandates that one should not spy on others.

## Right of freedom

According to Islam, no one besides God can limit human freedom which includes freedom of religion and worship for both believers and non-believers. Since it is a God given right, no ruler or legislative body has the right to take away the right to freedom.

Islam does not allow anyone to be imprisoned unless guilt has been proved. An accused, who has the right to defend himself, is guaranteed a fair and impartial trial. Since each individual person is responsible for his own actions, a person cannot be arrested for a crime that someone else may have committed.

## Right to protest against tyranny

A citizen of an Islamic state has the right to protest against tyranny by the ruler or government. This right cannot be taken away through legislation or by an executive order. The first caliph, Abu Bakr, is reported to have said, "Cooperate with me when I am right but correct me when I commit error; obey me so long as I follow the commandments of Allah and His prophet; but turn away from me when I deviate."

## Right to freedom of thought and expression

Islam recognizes the right of freedom of thought and expression. However, there is one condition that it imposes on this particular right. It cannot be used to propagate any vice or evil that is considered harmful for society.

Islam is very clear about freedom of conscience and conviction. If a Muslim disagrees with a law being implemented, he has the right to protest. If he believes the law is un-Islamic, he can even refuse to comply with it. Islam also allows a person the freedom to choose without being subject to coercion. This right is guaranteed in the Koran, which states that there can be no compulsion in religion.

## Right to justice

According to the Koran, "The most honored of you in the sight of Allah is (he who is) the most righteous of you." Righteousness consists of both belief and actions that are just. The Koran makes clear that righteousness determines merit—not factors such as social status, wealth, power or gender. It highlights both the right to seek justice and the duty to do justice. According to Islam, justice cannot be denied even to those who are hated. Committing injustice is considered to be one of the worst sins in Islam.

## Right to life's basic necessities

Islam recognizes that there are some people in every society who are disadvantaged, destitute, and needy. Therefore, it has provided such people the right to be helped by those who are more fortunate. Hence, it encourages the giving of charity and also made mandatory zakat a pillar of Islam.

## Right to equality

According to Islamic law, all citizens are equal in every respect and no one is above the law. There should be absolutely no difference in the way an ordinary Muslim citizen, a non-Muslim citizen, or the ruler should be treated. A society that fails to provide equal justice flouts the basic Islamic concept of equality.

## Political rights

Every citizen is granted political rights which includes the right to participate in the affairs of the state. Citizens need to be consulted regarding how the government is run. Even Muhammad[P] was commanded to seek counsel from his companions, "Consult with them upon the conduct of affairs (3:159)." Members of the legislature and Shoora must be elected by the citizens. They can stay in power only so long as they retain the confidence of the electorate.

## Minority rights

Islam recognizes the rights of non-Muslims living in an Islamic state and grants them protection. Their life, property, and honor are to be respected and protected just like Muslims. Additionally, non-Muslims are provided complete freedom of conscience and belief. In civil and criminal matters, Islam does not distinguish between a Muslim and a non-Muslim.

## Right to respect

According to Islam, man is considered to be God's vicegerent on earth. He has been provided with intelligence and the ability to exercise freedom of choice. Also, among all the creatures that God created, man was given the highest status and, with it, the right to be respected.

## Right to work

The right to work is a fundamental right that is guaranteed by Islam. According to the Koran, every person has the right to work and enjoy the fruits of his labor. Islam encourages one to work and earn a living to take care of one's own self, wife, children, parents, siblings, and the disadvantaged. Depending on others, for those who are able to work, is highly discouraged.

# CHAPTER 10
# WOMEN

## BACKGROUND

### Status of Arabian women before Islam

The condition of women in Arabia was pathetic before Muhammad[P] started preaching Islam in 610. The following are some aspects of their condition at that time:

- ❑ Women had practically no independent rights
- ❑ Birth of a girl was considered a misfortune and a threat to family honor
- ❑ New-born girls were buried alive
- ❑ A woman could be traded like a commodity

### Role played by women in Islam

Muhammad[P]'s first convert was his first wife, Khadijah. She provided the initial moral support, when he received his first revelation, and continued providing it during the difficult Meccan persecution period till she died in 619. Ayesha, also Muhammad[P]'s wife, became a scholar and is one of the best Hadith sources. Over 2,200 Hadith have been attributed to her. Only two other sources have been credited with more Hadith than Ayesha.

Ayesha was considered to be a fountain of knowledge and an expert in religious affairs and politics. She was highly respected and her advice was eagerly sought by Muslims. Ayesha took an active part in politics, including pressuring Caliph Ali to take action against the murderers of his predecessor—Caliph

Uthman. Muhammad[P]'s daughter, Fatima, played an important role in propagating Islam. Rabia Basri has been known as a great scholar in Islamic history.

There have been many female Muslim rulers including:
- Egyptian Mamluk Shajar al-Durr, wife of Salahuddin's nephew, who repelled the crusader attack led by Louis IX of France
- Abish, the last ruler of the "House of Salghar," who ruled the province of Fars during the Mongol period
- Razia Sultana of India, a brave warrior and capable administrator, who ruled India for almost four years

Many other Muslim women have left their mark on art and literature, as well as politics, including Noorjehan and Zaib un-Nisa.

## Recent deterioration in treatment

With the decline of the Islamic civilization, the status and condition of women also started to deteriorate. In the past two centuries, the condition of Muslims deteriorated considerably and hit rock bottom. In tandem with that decline, the status of women suffered considerably and so did the implementation of their rights. They also became victims of the "culturalization of Islam." It resulted in women being poorly treated according to local and tribal traditions, many of which were discriminatory against women. In many societies, which were predominantly Muslim, local and tribal traditions came to be incorrectly associated with Islam even though, in many cases, such traditions were either un-Islamic or not required by Islam. Examples of such customs include:
- Female circumcision—a tribal custom in Africa
- Reverse dowry—whereby men are paid cash in order to marry girls, who are considered a burden due to their gender
- Lighting of lamps at shrines and graves—a pagan and Hindu tradition in India
- Burqa—in Afghanistan and parts of the Indian subcontinent

Since there is a lot of fiction that is intertwined with facts, there is widespread misperception about the status and rights that Islam has granted women—not just in the West but even in Islamic countries.

# WHAT ISLAM PROVIDED WOMEN

## Removed stigma and false notions

Islam clarified some wrong notions about women dating back to the time that Adam disobeyed God. According to Islam, Adam was tempted by Satan—not Eve. Since both Adam and Eve disobeyed God, women cannot be considered the source of evil. Islam holds women in high respect as is reflected in the high status and rights that have been bestowed upon them. It provides great respect for women such as Eve, Mary (mother of Jesus) and Haggar (wife of Abraham). The importance of Mary (Maryam) can be gauged from the fact that an important chapter of the Koran is named after her.

## Rights women had been denied

The introduction of Islam in Arabia marked a sudden change in the status of women. They were elevated to a prestigious position where they were considered to be spiritually and intellectually equal to men. They were provided the same rights as were enjoyed by men. They were also provided with the status of individuals in their own right. Due to Islam, women also obtained the right to:

❏   Own and dispose of property and earnings
❏   Choose a husband
❏   Be supported by the husband—even if the wife is wealthy
❏   Be supported by a male relative, if required

❑ Inherit property from parents, husband, son, brother or even grandson
❑ Keep her wealth after marriage
❑ Spend her own money as desired
❑ Retain maiden name
❑ Divorce
❑ Remarry
❑ Participate in political affairs and vote
❑ Receive an education
❑ Be protected against defamation

Along with their rights, women also have the same obligations as men. They have to obey the same commandments regarding prayers, fasting, Hajj, etc., with some minor exceptions. However, in return for their additional responsibilities, men have been given the leadership at home while women have been designated as the guardians of the household. Though men are assigned the leadership at home, they have also been instructed to treat women with kindness and love—and not to dominate them.

## Recognition as an independent identity

A woman in Islam is considered to be an independent identity. She will be judged by God, just like any man, based on her individual performance in this world. Her beliefs, actions and conduct will determine her ultimate success or failure on the Day of Judgment. According to Islam, righteousness will determine every human's fate—not the gender.

## Recognition as a legal entity

In Islam, a woman is recognized as an independent legal entity. She can:
❑ Own individual property
❑ Inherit property

❑ Dispose of property
❑ Run a business

## Equality with men

In Islam, men and women are considered to be equal. They have the same rights and obligations such as prayers, fasting, zakat, and Hajj. Both men and women are expected to perform good deeds and avoid evil. They are also judged by the same moral yardstick. The same rewards and punishments apply to men and women. On the Day of Judgment, both will be judged only according to their deeds and righteousness.

While providing equality, Islam also divides responsibilities between men and women based on their differences. For example, women are responsible for developing a God-conscious and righteous atmosphere at home, while men are responsible for the financial needs of the family. A woman can work outside the home and contribute to the family income. However, the ultimate financial responsibility has been assigned to the husband.

## Consideration and provision for differences

While Islam considers men and women equal, and they will be judged as such, it does make provision for their differences. The following are some examples:

❑ A man inherits double of what a woman inherits; however, he is financially responsible for his family and any female relatives who might fall on bad times
❑ Both men and women are required to dress modestly; however, women have a more restrictive dress code due to their greater ability to attract; Islam tries to avoid creating the conditions that can lead to any impermissible act

❑ Women get exclusive custody over children till they reach puberty
❑ Women are exempted from daily prayers and fasting during menstrual periods, pregnancy, and when nursing an infant; however, they can make up the missed fasts at a later time
❑ Friday congregational prayer is mandatory for men but not for women

The position of women, in terms of status, can be gauged from two Hadith. A man asked Muhammad[P], "Who is most entitled to be treated with the best companionship with me?" He responded, "Your mother." The man again asked, "Who is next?" Muhammad[P] repeated his answer, "Your mother." When the man repeated his question, the Prophet also repeated his response, "Your mother." When the man again repeated the question, "Who is next?", Muhammad[P] answered, "Your father ." On another occasion, Muhammad[P] is reported to have told a man, "Stay with her (mother), for paradise is at her feet."

## Same relationship with God

The Koran, on numerous occasions, speaks of both men and women in the same tone, such as "for believing men and women who give charity, for men and women who fast, for men and women who guard their chastity." In Islam, there is no difference between men and women in their relationship with God. Both men and women are instructed to follow the same commands. They are promised the same rewards and punishments which, for both, will be based on the same criteria.

# WOMEN AND FAMILY LIFE

## Status of marriage in Islam

In Islam, marriage is very strongly encouraged. Besides its primary objective, of establishing a family, it also helps keep away evils such as promiscuity and fornication. Muhammad[P] is reported to have said, "Marriage is my Sunnah" and "Whosoever keeps away from it is not from me."

## Divorce

An Islamic marriage is not a sacrament. Rather, it is a contract, recommended to be in writing, which can be terminated by either party. Despite that permission, divorces are not common among Muslims, though they have started to increase in recent years. According to the Hadith, while divorce is allowed by Islam, it is also viewed as most hated among the permissions that have been given to Muslims by God. It is also believed to be Satan's most loved action.

## Prerequisites for marriage

For marriage to take place, the consent of both the man and woman are required. Marriage is deemed to be mandatory for a healthy man who can meet two conditions:
- Means to pay mahr or dowry
- Ability to support a wife and children

Mahr is the dowry, or gift, that a man is required to give his wife when the marriage takes place. The amount is mutually agreed upon before marriage and, if the wife wants to, can be forgiven. The amount, which is influenced by the social status and earning ability of the bridegroom, as well as local traditions, can vary from under a hundred dollar to tens of thousands of dollars.

According to some schools of thought, marriage becomes mandatory if a man thinks that he cannot avoid fornication. It also becomes compulsory for a woman who fears that she may fall into sin unless she marries.

## Roles and responsibilities of husband and wife

The rules and regulations governing family life for Muslims are defined by the Sharia. The man is responsible, as the leader of the family, to provide for its financial needs while the woman is responsible for household affairs and the children's upbringing. A woman is expected to obey her husband unless she is asked to disobey God. In such a case, she can refuse to obey.

A man, on his part, must be considerate and caring. He must respect and honor his wife. According to the Hadith, "The best among you is he who is the most kind to his wife and I am the kindest amongst you to my wives." Since Muhammad[P] is the example and role model who must be followed by Muslims, this Hadith indicates the importance of being kind to one's wife.

Both husband and wife are required to be diligent about their responsibilities to each other and be faithful to each other. However, despite their different roles and responsibilities, men and women are considered equal in the eyes of God.

## Marriage ceremony

There are no elaborate rituals associated with a Muslim marriage ceremony. Anyone can perform the ceremony, though it is usually done by a religious scholar or an imam in the presence of two witnesses. The ceremony involves confirming the consent of the bride and groom, stating the simple marriage wows, imam's short sermon and recitation of a few verses of the Koran and, finally, prayers for a happy and successful marriage.

## Marriage with non-Muslims

A Muslim man is allowed to marry a Christian or Jewish woman. However, he cannot marry an unbelieving woman. A Muslim woman is not allowed to marry a non-Muslim man. There are a few reasons, which can be causes of conflict after such a marriage, for this prohibition:

❑ Islam guarantees freedom of religion to the non-Muslim wife of a Muslim man. However, other religions do not provide the same freedom. Hence, a Muslim woman runs the risk of being denied permission to practice her religion if she marries a non-Muslim.

❑ Historically, children have followed their father's religion. Therefore, a Muslim woman marrying into a non-Muslim family will see her children being raised as non-Muslims.

❑ A Christian or Jewish woman marrying a Muslim man comes into a home where her prophet is revered and respected. However, such a situation does not exist when a Muslim woman marries a non-Muslim man who does not believe in, or respect, Muhammad[P] and Islam.

# MUSLIM WOMEN'S ISSUES IN THE MODERN WORLD

## Women's rights are paid lip service

There is a big disconnect between how Islam perceives women and how they are actually treated in Muslim societies. On paper, Muslim women have many rights that they have been granted by Islam. However, in practical terms, due to the way Muslim societies are organized and run, the overwhelming majority of women hardly ever get the opportunity of exercising many of their rights. For example, in matters of inheritance, they often get short changed. Neither do they have the freedom to freely choose their spouses. Also, education is not deemed necessary for them in many societies.

In many communities where women are shabbily treated and their rights are denied, ignorance and local customs can be blamed. In many countries such as Afghanistan, people sincerely but incorrectly believe that their customs, especially pertaining to women, are sanctioned by Islam. Also, in many male-dominated Muslim societies, even though there is awareness of Islamic women's rights and lip service is paid to them, such rights are not implemented for a variety of reasons.

## Ignorance and lack of education

Lack of education is a problem that is pervasive among Muslims—both men and women. However, the problem is far more widespread and serious for women than it is for men. In most Islamic societies, knowledge of Islam, for the overwhelming majority of Muslims, is limited to the basic acts of worship. Lack of education has bred ignorance, which has been inherited for many generations now. The consequences of a lack of education are apparent everywhere, especially in the way women are treated in the name of Islam. A prime example is Afghanistan, where the Taliban prohibited girls from attending schools. The Taliban were supposed to be well-versed in Islam and, yet, they implemented a policy that is totally against the teachings of Islam. The first word in the Koran, whose instructions Muslims are expected to implement, is "Read!" There is no sentence or verse in the Koran which indicates that reading, and what it implies, should be restricted to men.

## Mistreatment

Even a cursory study of the Koran, or the Hadith, will reveal that women are given a very high status in Islam. Again and again, men are exhorted to treat their women well and to be kind to them. However, despite such instructions, women in many Islamic societies are oppressed or mistreated even by those who are perceived to be "religious." Partial implementation of Islam, which suits such people, clouds but does not change the fact that Islam has provided wide-ranging rights to women and that it does not, in any way, condone their mistreatment.

## Forced arranged marriages

Islam requires that the consent of the woman, who has been given the authority to choose a husband of her choice, be obtained for her marriage. However, in some Islamic communities, the environment is such that it is difficult for a girl to say no to a match proposed by her parents. Refusal to agree to a marriage proposal put forward by the family can, in some communities, lead to serious consequences that are driven by cultural rather than Islamic considerations. They can range from verbal abuse to outright honor killing of the girl—as happens in some tribal areas. Such extreme actions, in regions where such acts are carried out, are typically widespread among the adherents of all religions and not restricted to Muslims.

## Misuse of the right to polygamy

During the early years of Islam, Muslims had to fight many wars in which they were heavily outnumbered. Many young fighters were killed, which was one of the primary reasons why men were allowed to have more than one wife. Such permission prevented many widows from being forced into prostitution which, prior to Islam, would have been their only option since other income producing opportunities for women were unavailable during those times. Additionally, it provided protection and benefits for the widow's children.

Islam allows a man to have four wives However, there are conditions attached to the permission for polygamy. The man has to treat all his wives fairly, equally, and with perfect justice. If he buys a house for one, he has to buy a house for each wife. According to the Koran, "You will never be able to do perfect justice between wives even if it is your ardent desire…(4:129)." In other words, there is discouragement in that verse as it indicates that man may fall into sin by not being just. However, many Muslims who do practice polygamy conveniently ignore the attached conditions of equal treatment and fairness.

## Female genital mutilation

This is a pre-Islamic tribal practice common in some African countries and is not based on any Islamic teaching. Some African tribes are practicing this barbaric cultural practice even after their conversion to Islam.

## Common misconceptions

There are many misconceptions and myths about the status and role of women in Islam, especially among non-Muslims. In too many cases, cultural practices are believed to be Islamic practices, which they are not. The following is a list of some common and incorrect misconceptions:

❑ Women cannot work outside the home
❑ Polygamy is strongly recommended
❑ Men have a higher status than women
❑ Women are not allowed to have an education
❑ Women cannot take part in political affairs
❑ Women cannot divorce their husbands
❑ Women are not allowed to drive
❑ Honor killing of women is allowed

# CHAPTER 11
# SECTARIAN AND EXTERNAL DIFFERENCES

## SECTARIAN DIVISIONS AND JURISPRUDENCE

### Diversity and splits in Islam

The followers of Islam, estimated to be about 1.2 billion, are dispersed throughout the world. They are anything but homogeneous and are split into two major sects—Sunni and Shia. These, in turn, contain sub-sects and overall, by some counts, there are 72 sects. The Sunnis account for about 90 percent of Muslims, while Shias account for the remaining ten percent. Most of the Shias are concentrated in Iran, Iraq, and the Indian subcontinent.

### Sunni

The Sunnis derive their name from the word "Sunnah", which means following the sayings and actions of Muhammad[P]. Sunnis are the mainstream orthodox Muslims who follow traditional Islam. Their beliefs are the ones that have been described in this book.

Sunnis believe that they should be governed by consensus and, consequently, ruled by a ruler whose election must be based on democratic principles. They do not believe that an individual needs or requires any clergy, or other intermediaries, to establish a relationship with God.

## Shia

The Shia Muslims split from mainstream Islam over an emotional dispute concerning Muhammad<sup>P</sup>'s successor. They believe that Ali ibn Abu Talib should have been made the caliph after his death. However, the community successively selected three others as caliph—Abu Bakr, Umar and Uthman—before Ali was ultimately selected as the fourth caliph. The key event defining the Shia-Sunni split occurred when Hussein, who was the younger son of Ali and the grandson of Prophet Muhammad<sup>P</sup>, and his family were massacred by the Ummayyad army of Yezid at Karbala in Iraq.

The Shias believe that the leader of Islam should be a descendant of Ali. They believe that religious and political authority resides in the 12 imams or leaders who, starting with Ali, have led them since then. The imams are believed to be sinless and privy to knowledge that others do not have. The Shias believe that the last imam, Muhammad al-Mahdi, was born around 868 but never died. Instead, he went into hiding from human view and will appear at an opportune time.

The Shias are split into two main sects—"Twelvers" and "Ismailis." The former believe that there were a total of 12 imams, including the last one who went into hiding. They expect him to come back as the Messiah. The Twelvers have a clergy system that is organized in a hierarchy, with the ayatollah being at the highest level. The Ismailis have many sub-sects including the "Seveners", who believe that there were only seven imams and that the last one went into hiding.

The Shias have five fundamental religious beliefs. They are monotheism, prophethood, vicegerency (imamate), justice, and Day of Judgment. Shias believe that their clergy is empowered to interpret God's will. Their theology is characterized by its glorification of Ali and his son, Hussein. In Shiaism, there is a strong theme of martyrdom and suffering.

## Reform and other movements

There are a number of sects, or sub-sects, and reform movements that have originated from mainstream Islam. The most prominent among them include the Wahhabis and the Sufis.

### Wahhabis

Muhammad ibn Abd al-Wahhab, who died in 1792, was a religious scholar and reformer in Arabia. The objective of his movement was to establish Islamic practice as it existed during the time of Muhammad[P]. He wanted to purge local practices, many of which were un-Islamic, that had crept into the practice of Islam. Such practices included visiting shrines, asking saints to intercede with God, etc. He preached against the introduction of any innovations and adherence to the original Islamic teachings. He focused on the principle of the oneness of God and reiterated that God did not share His powers with any imam or saint.

In 1744, Abd al-Wahhab and Muhammad ibn Saud, a political leader, decided to join forces to establish a state based on Islamic principles. The religious and political combination proved a potent one. It led to the ultimate establishment, throughout Arabia, of Wahhabism and the rule of the Saud family. At this time, the Wahhabis dominate the Arabian peninsula.

### Kharajites

The Kharajites, who account for less than one percent of all Muslims, trace their origin to the followers of Ali. When Muawiyah challenged Ali's election as the caliph, it led to war between them. When they stopped fighting and appointed an arbitrator, part of Ali's army rejected the compromise attempt and left him in 657. The ones who left were known as the "Kharajis" or "the ones who leave." Ali was subsequently murdered by a Kharajite in 661. The Kharajites continued to oppose the next caliph, Muawiyah, when he succeeded Ali.

The Kharajites follow the Koran and Sunnah very strictly. They believe that profession of faith must be accompanied by righteousness and good deeds. The Kharajites are characterized by a fanatical belief in equality, idealistic views of justice, and piety. They have had a very strong tendency to punish those who deviate from Muhammad[P]'s teachings.

### Sufism

Sufism, which developed in the tenth century, is not strictly a sect or a school of thought. It is a spiritual way of removing desires such as jealousy, envy, pride, etc. Sufis can be found among both Shias and Sunnis. Sufism emphasizes personal piety and mysticism. Its mystical traditions seek inner knowledge directly from God through meditation and rituals. Typically, Sufis emphasize spirituality, engage in prayers, and repeat phrases glorifying God. They believe, along with some other non-Sufi scholars, that the Koran can be interpreted in many ways. The Sufis, who believe in the hidden and mystical interpretation of the Koran, refer to them as "wisdom", "indication" or "hints." For many Sufis, their ascetic life is characterized by deprivation and meditation. Many Sufis played a missionary role in converting people to Islam, in newer lands, and helping them integrate their beliefs and practices into it.

### Other fringe movements

There are a number of splinter groups that have spun off from Islam. The Bahai, who are concentrated in Iran, initially attempted to integrate the world's religions but, later on, developed into a new religion. The Ahmadiyya movement in India believes that its founder was a Messiah and that Muhammad[P] was not the last prophet sent by God. Mainstream followers of Islam consider their beliefs blasphemous and, therefore, do not consider Ahmadiyyas to be Muslims.

The Nation of Islam Black Muslim movement started in the America as an anti-white movement. It teaches that blacks are superior to whites. It also taught that Elijah Muhammad[P] was a prophet of God and Wallace Fard was God incarnate. Hence, even though they use the name Islam, the Nation of Islam is un-Islamic and cannot be associated with orthodox Islam. Malcolm X was a Nation of Islam leader who reversed his racist anti-white beliefs after performing Hajj. He rejected the Nation of Islam beliefs, once he realized what Islam really taught, and joined mainstream orthodox Islam.

## Schools of Thought (Jurisprudence)

As Islam expanded beyond the Arabian Peninsula, it faced unique and complex issues, many of which did not have explicit answers in the Koran and the Hadith. Therefore, there arose a need for the practical application of Islamic laws in an environment that had changed considerably since the days of Muhammad[P]. That requirement led to the development of various schools of thought that interpreted and applied Islamic principles to issues in virtually all aspects of life.

### Sunni Jurisprudence

The Sunnis have four major schools of thought named after their founders—who were eminent scholars. The schools are:
- Hanafi—named after Abu Hanifa
- Maliki—named after Malik ibn Anas

❑  Shafi'i—named after Muhammad ibn Idris Shafi'i
❑  Hanbali—named after Ahmad ibn Muhammad ibn Hanbal

A Sunni can follow any one of these four schools of thought. However, the generally accepted principle is to follow a single school. The other schools are used in the search for an answer only if the school being followed fails to provide an answer.

## Shia Jurisprudence

The Shias follow the Jafri school of thought. Even though there are differences, the Sunnis and the Shias:
❑  Have the same basic beliefs
❑  Follow the Koran and Muhammad[P]
❑  Believe in the five pillars of Islam

The major differences between the Shias and Sunnis lie in their leadership and in the interpretation of the Koran. The Shias believe that the sayings of Ali ibn Abu Talib should be as authoritative as the Sunnah. However, Sunnis do not agree with that belief.

The Sunnis believe in implementing the letter of the Koran. However, the Shias look to the spirit (hidden) rather than the letter (apparent) of the Koran. It is due to that reason that the Shia religious leadership plays a significant role in the interpretation of the Koran and, also, how it is viewed by the Shia rank and file.

# BELIEFS ABOUT JESUS

## Birth and crucifixion

Islam teaches that Jesus was born to Mary, who was a virgin. The creation of Jesus, who had no father, is compared in the Koran to the creation of Adam, who had neither mother nor father.

Muslims do not believe that Jesus was crucified. They believe that God saved, and raised, him and that someone else was crucified in his place. They also believe that Jesus will return before the Day of Judgment. However, he will not come back as a prophet with a new message. Instead, he will follow the religion Islam taught by Muhammad[P]. His mission will be to destroy evil and kill the false Messiah—the anti-Christ.

## Jesus is only a prophet

According to Islam, Jesus is only a prophet. The message that he taught was the same that was delivered by the prophets and messengers who came before him: Adam, Noah, Abraham, Moses, and others. His message, of monotheism and the oneness of God, was subsequently delivered by Muhammad[P].

Muslims believe that Jesus had the power of miracles and that he was the promised Messiah of the Jews, who rejected him. According to Islam, the Christian belief that he is the son of God is equivalent to polytheism and a rejection of what Jesus had taught his own followers. Muslims firmly reject the concept of Trinity—Father, Son, and Holy Ghost.

## Highest regard for Jesus

Islam respects and honors all prophets and messengers sent by God, including Jesus. He is held in high regard by Muslims and considered to be one of the most important prophets. Whenever Muslims speak the name of Jesus, they respectfully add the phrase "Peace be upon him."

## New Testament

Muslims believe that the Gospel is the scripture that contains God's revelations to Jesus. However, the scripture available at this time is not authentic due to additions and deletions that took place over time and, hence, it cannot be used as a guide by Muslims.

# COMPARING BELIEFS WITH OTHER RELIGIONS

## Evolution of Islam

According to its followers, Islam started with the first prophet—Adam. The Islamic lesson of "surrender to God", which was first preached by Adam, continued to be taught by subsequent prophets including Moses and Jesus. However, while their teachings were appropriate at the time that they preached, they needed to be updated with the passage of time. God took care of that need by sending more prophets who brought modified messages that were appropriate for their times. The final message was sent through Muhammad[P] who finalized the religion of Islam for all times to come. Therefore, Judaism and Christianity are viewed as incomplete versions of Islam that were replaced by the final version introduced by Muhammad[P].

## Monotheism

The following are the main fundamental differences that Judaism and Christianity have with Islam, as perceived by its followers:
- ❑ Judaism has compromised monotheism by elevating the opinions and interpretations of rabbis to the level of God
- ❑ Christianity has compromised monotheism by viewing Jesus as the son of God

## Belief in prophets and scriptures

Islam is the only religion that teaches its followers that they must believe in the earlier prophets, messengers, and scriptures. Without this fundamental belief, they cannot be considered Muslims. However, Christianity and Judaism followers do not believe in Islam or Muhammad[P], despite signs given to them of the coming of Muhammad[P].

## Concept of a chosen people

Islam firmly rejects the concept of a chosen race or people. Muslims are taught very clearly that all human beings are equal. According to Islam, there can be no superiority based upon color, race, gender, nationality, tribe or any other criteria except righteousness.

## Original sin

Islam does not believe in original sin. According to it, all humans are born innocent and free of sin. Adam committed a sin but he repented and was forgiven. Islam does not believe that someone else has to pay for a sin, especially when the very person who committed it, Adam, was forgiven. According to Islam, every person is accountable for his or her own actions. Therefore, there is no need to be saved from the "inherent" sin.

## Salvation

According to Islam, salvation is acquired by performing good deeds, not through the mediation of a savior. Salvation will be the reward for those who believe in one God and follow His commandments. Muslims do not believe that salvation is dependent upon the following incorrect beliefs:

❑ Resurrection of Jesus
❑ Believing that Jesus was the son of God
❑ Through confessing sins

## Ultimate admittance to heaven or hell

Muslims believe that on the Day of Judgment, all the good and bad deeds of a person will be weighed. According to the Koran, "He who has done an atom's weight of good shall see it (99:7)." It also states, "He who has done an atom's weight of evil shall see it (99:8)." Based upon the preponderance of good or bad deeds, a person will be sent to heaven or hell. In Islam, there is no concept of purgatory.

## Church and State

Christianity is a religion that limits itself to religious practice. Islam is a way of life that encompasses all facets of a man's life including personal, social, political, and religious. Islam regulates the complete life of a society and, therefore, it does not recognize the separation of church and state.

# ATTITUDE TOWARDS OTHER RELIGIONS

## View of other religions and their followers

Islam classifies other religions into two groups: They are:
- [ ] People of the Book
- [ ] Other religions

Christians as well as Jews are viewed as "People of the Book" with whom Muslims share the most important common belief, monotheism, as well as many others. Muslims view the prophets of the Jews and Christians, Moses and Jesus, as among the greatest prophets. A Muslim has to consider them prophets as part of his fundamental beliefs.

Many Muslims believe that those who believe in the concept of Trinity are not Christians and, therefore, should be classified as non-believers. Their reasoning is that such followers are in denial of Jesus' fundamental message—oneness of God. Such people, according to Muslims, fall in the second category (other religions).

In Islamic societies, Jews and Christians are allowed full religious freedom. Since they are considered "People of the Book", a Muslim man can marry a Christian or a Jewish woman.

## Attitude towards followers of other religions

Muslims have been commanded by the Koran not to use force to convert anyone. It enjoins complete religious freedom to non-Muslims. There are clear and unambiguous commandments for Muslims to protect non-Muslim citizens in an Islamic society. Non-Muslims have been guaranteed freedom of worship as well as protection of life, property, and religious sites by Islam. Islam also teaches that Jews and Christians should be respected—as they are believers (People of the Book). There should be complete justice for them, even as minorities.

Though there have been wars and animosity between Muslims and Jews, Muslims are often reminded of their high point in their relationship with them. It occurred when Umar, the second caliph, captured Jerusalem but allowed complete religious freedom for Christians. He also permitted Jews, who had previously been denied entry by the Christians, to re-enter Jerusalem.

The relationship between Jews and Muslims had been good in Palestine, where they had lived side by side for centuries, till the creation of Israel. In recent times, almost all the Jews in the Middle East countries migrated to Israel. Therefore, there is practically no daily interaction between Muslims and Jews except in Occupied Palestine, where there is considerable animosity between them for obvious reasons.

Despite past animosity due to the Crusades, relations between Muslims and Christians at this time are good except in a few isolated areas. In many countries, they are natural partners on various issues such as abortion, homosexuality, and other moral issues.

# INDEX